WITH MY WHOLE HEART

D0588213

To Sarah,
without whose love and faithfulness
my heart would have failed,
and
for Harriet, Jemima and Tabitha

WITH MY WHOLE HEART

Reflections on the heart of the Psalms

James Jones

First published in Great Britain in 2012

Society for Promoting Christian Knowledge
36 Causton Street
London SW1P 4ST
www.spckpublishing.co.uk

Copyright © James Jones 2012

All rights reserved. No part of this book may be reproduced or transmitted in any form
or by any means, electronic or mechanical, including photocopying, recording,
or by any information storage and retrieval system, without
permission in writing from the publisher.

SPCK does not necessarily endorse the individual views contained in its publications.

British Library Cataloguing-in-Publication Data
A catalogue record for this book is available from the British Library

ISBN 978–0–281–06805–0
eBook ISBN 978–0–281–06806–7

Typeset by Graphicraft Ltd, Hong Kong
First printed in Great Britain by Ashford Colour Press
Subsequently digitally printed in Great Britain

Contents

Contents

Contents

Acknowledgements

Special thanks to Margaret, Wendy, Chris, Tom and Phil.

Prelude to the Psalms

On a certain Tuesday I was on my feet in the House of Lords asking a question about the future of the Community Justice Centre in Liverpool. As I sat down I could feel my heart pumping and a pain in my chest.

On the Wednesday I was at the Heart and Chest Hospital in Liverpool doing a tread test after which the consultant said kindly and firmly, 'There's a problem.'

On Thursday I was having an angiogram after which, as I was lying on the table, he offered to show me the pictures. Being of a squeamish nature I declined. He leant close sympathetically and said, 'You need surgery.' He kept me in, conferred with his team and transferred me to his colleague who operated first thing on Monday.

That weekend became something of a retreat in which I prepared for the operation both physically and spiritually.

As I said my prayers and read psalms from the Book of Common Prayer, whose poetry adds fathoms to their theological depth, I was arrested by two verses in Psalm 27: 'I should utterly have fainted' (That's me! I thought): 'but that I believe verily to see the goodness of the Lord in the land of the living' (That's me, I hope). 'O tarry thou the Lord's leisure: be strong, and he shall comfort thine heart; and put thou thy trust in the Lord' (vv. 15, 16).

In the weeks that followed the surgery the psalms not only kept me company day and night (especially in the early hours of restlessness) but also spoke to my heart in many ways, and of the heart. These are some of the reflections based on each occasion the word 'heart' occurs in the psalms. They are necessarily short. Brevity was all that I was capable of as I recuperated. Writing them became part of my rule of life and, if truth be told, part of my therapy. I hope the reader will excuse any self-indulgence!

I am conscious that I owe my life to the medical team at Liverpool's Heart and Chest Hospital. It's one of the finest in the country with an international reputation. Mr Brian Fabri my surgeon and Mr David Ramsdale my cardiologist and their colleagues are all that any patient could hope for. Skilled, sensitive, authoritative and encouraging. I write these pages constantly aware of how much they, along with my GP and friend Dr George Kuruvilla, have done for me.

I am also fortified like many patients by the love of family and friends and in my case the fellowship of the Diocese of Liverpool whose prayers have sustained me throughout. It is an extraordinary privilege to be a bishop and to be prayed for daily by brothers and sisters. My gratitude is exceeded only by my sense of unworthiness.

It is my heart's desire that this little book would take the reader to the Psalms, to the Book of Common Prayer, to the Bible and thereby into the courts of the Lord.

> Yea, the sparrow hath found her an house, and the swallow
> a nest where she may lay her young: even thy altars, O Lord
> of hosts, my King and my God.   (Psalm 84.3)

Any commentary on the psalms will seem pedestrian by comparison with the poetry of the Prayer Book. Explanation can never reach the depths touched by poetry's verse and vision.

I remember at college the Oxford theologian G. B. Caird, in his lectures on the New Testament, telling us that unpacking a parable had about as much force as explaining a joke. The moment you try it the power escapes. The same must be true of the psalms. So I hope you will forgive my musings should they spoil your reading and, if they do, go straight to the psalm via the chosen verse.

I'm aware too in offering these reflections that readers will be at different places in their belief in God. So, before we take off, let me build a runway out of my own reasons for believing. There are ten: Creation, Conscience, the Commandments, the Covenant, the Course of history, Christ, the Cross, Communion, the Church and the Canon of Scripture. I know these will weigh variously with different people, yet it is in their cumulative value that I find persuasion.

Creation

The beauty and balance of the natural world, notwithstanding the reality of being 'red in tooth and claw', evoke from deep within a sense of awe and of a greatness greater than oneself. This greatness is manifestly alive and dynamic, neither inanimate nor dead.

Conscience

Out of the mouths of even infants come the words, 'That's not fair!' Throughout life we make judgements about what is fair and unfair regarding the behaviour of other people as if there were some moral code that was binding not just on ourselves but on them too. Of course, this sense of justice could be illusory, but if so it would confound the experience of billions of people who readily use such phrases. Conscience is universal. It suggests there is an intuited law which is objective and binding on all.

Commandments

The law that our conscience intuits is made explicit in the Commandments. There is no society that holds that lying is better than telling the truth, betrayal better than trust, hatred better than love. Of course, the survival of any society depends on its members abiding by such a code. The moral law is a given for the human family and bears the authority of the Giver. And the Ten Commandments root this right conduct in a right relationship with the Giver of the law.

Covenant

The relationship between the Creator and the human family and all Creation is set out in the Bible in covenants. Many people believe that there is something behind the universe, even a force. Yet what we value most as human beings is to be able to love and to be loved. It is logical to imagine that the Creator can do at least all that we are capable of. Hence, it is not a giant step to believing that behind the universe is not something, but someone who can love and be loved. Such is the covenant of love between Creator and humanity.

The Course of history

Although the landscape of history is scarred with battles and bloodshed and sometimes tragically in the name of religion, there appears a progressive march through history from enslavement to freedom. It is as if humanity through all its struggles is destined to be free. There seems to be a motif of freedom marbled into the human heart that takes us beyond ourselves to an ordained destiny of liberation.

Christ

Philosophers, poets, songwriters and students seek the truth about our existence. In answer to the quest after truth God gives us not a set of abstract propositions about the truth but a true person. All that we might imagine God to be on earth we see in Jesus. Hearing him pray and meeting him alive after his death persuaded his followers that he was the Son of God.

The Cross

The love that conquers all is the love that can forgive even its enemies. When they drove nails through such love the assassins heard their victim pray for their forgiveness, a forgiveness that embraces the whole human family. This is supernatural love.

Communion

It is through personal experience that we prove things to be true. The Spirit of Christ comes to those who ask. It is in the asking and in the coming that we begin to change and to see the world differently, as if we had been born again.

The Church

For all its faults and foibles, for all its betrayals of the truest human being to walk the earth, there is an irrepressible essence seen in the life of ordinary believers who display extraordinary grace. When you meet them it is impossible to gainsay the integrity of their faith.

The Canon of Scripture

The story of the collection of texts that make up the Bible is so complex you cannot attribute it to any single human being. Yet through the complexity and some apparent contradictions there is a story, surprising yet authoritatively consistent, that in spite of everything God loves the world. And so much so that he entered it and became one of us and one with us 'from the womb to the tomb'. Why? That for love's sake we might get a life that is fulfilling and everlasting.

It is the cumulation of these ten that humbles me to pray, 'Lord, I believe; help thou mine unbelief' (Mark 9.24 KJV). I know that volumes have been written on each of the above. The succinct rehearsal of them, however, on a miniature scale helps the reader to see in one viewing how much God has laid before us and to hear, in effect, how much God speaks to us in Creation, Conscience, Commandments, Covenant, history's Course, Christ, the Cross, Communion, the Church and the Canon of Scripture. It is a cumulative case that invites interrogation intellectually. But when all is said and done and debated there is an appeal not just to the mind but to the heart, to the will. The question eventually turns from, 'Can you believe?' to, 'Will you?'

It was to my heart, my will, that these psalms spoke in a crisis. I pray they will speak to your heart too.

And finally a postscript about the Book of Common Prayer. For the last 30 years, since I was a lay Reader, I have been an advocate of 'all-age worship'. Yet all of that time and before, since I was a server helping in the service of Holy Communion, I have loved the Book of Common Prayer. The glory of the Church of England lies in its breadth, holding together the classical and the contemporary. I served for a time on the Liturgical Commission under the exuberant, scholarly and generous chairing of Bishop David Stancliffe. With my children I was the originator of Eucharistic Prayer D in *Common Worship*.

I remain enthusiastic about welcoming children to the Lord's Table in ever new ways. But as, I hope, this small book shows, my heart continues to beat to the rhythm and cadences of the Book of Common Prayer. I trust the Church of England continues to find a place in her own heart for the liturgy and for the doctrine of her Prayer Book.

WITH MY WHOLE HEART

Psalm 4.4

Stand in awe, and sin not:
commune with your own heart, and in your chamber, and be still.

I would have thought that this invitation to communion would begin with a call to commune with God. But as we try to relate to God we need also to know ourselves, or at least to have some of our pretensions stripped away. This is seldom easy and sometimes painful and often happens against our will. As I was to discover in hospital, it is not unusual for a crisis to bring us to a point of reassessing our life, values, ambitions and relationships. For some of us it is only a crisis that will ever precipitate such a reassessment. And it is a very lonely place, especially when others seem unaffected by our struggles and the world goes on without us.

Communing with the heart is not a comfortable experience, not least when it takes place 'in your chamber', in the early hours of the morning when, as you lie sleepless on your bed, fears grow out of proportion, stalking your soul.

One response is to shut yourself down and try to banish the thoughts until dawn when daylight can cut them down to size. Another is to engage the heart in conversation and to confess to being a pygmy before these giants. Then, like some frightened animal frozen in the headlights, simply lie still before the enormity of all that haunts and daunts you.

Communing with the heart in such stillness may well bring to the surface many doubts and fears. But this is the fount of you, and the beginning of being real and true before God.

Pray

Lord,
this is me
full of fear:
hold me dear
to thee. Amen.

Psalm 4.8

Thou hast put gladness in my heart:
since the time that their corn, and wine, and oil, increased.

The bridge between communing with your own heart and the heart being gladdened is putting trust in God and basking in the light that shines out of him. But what is so delightful about this psalm and the promise of such gifts from God is the sheer earthiness of the gladness that God gives. It comes with an abundance of 'corn, and wine, and oil'. In other words, the heart finds joy in the material world.

You might have thought that the gladdening of the heart was a purely spiritual exercise. But this psalm holds together the spiritual and the material, for both are in the realm of God's providence. The light that shines from heaven and the fruit of the earth, the harvest of 'interaction between root and sky', make glad the heart in equal measure. I lost count of the number of well-wishers who assured me of the medicinal and spiritual benefits of a glass of red wine! And proved it with bottles!

Worship and prayer feed the soul. And so too do good food and fine wine, friendship, music, art and the wild orchestration of nature. Received as gifts, these tokens of God's affection enlarge the heart with the experience of grace, gifts given generously to the undeserving. They humble you, in a fit of thankful mystery: 'Why me?'

They lay a path for the prayer.

Pray

I will lay me down in peace, and take my rest: for it is thou, Lord, only, that makest me dwell in safety. (Psalm 4.9)

Psalm 7.10, 11

For the righteous God:
trieth the very hearts and reins.
My help cometh of God:
who preserveth them that are true of heart.

The character of God feels to me at times as if it were kept under a soundproof blanket. Just as well! He shudders in indignation at the unjust desecration of his creation and at the wanton destruction of any of his creatures. Yet we do not hear it.

For if God did not contain his pain and remain silent, which of us could bear to hear the roar of outrage that would deafen our universe? We often bemoan the silence of God, but perhaps it is the necessary and merciful condition of our survival in a world traumatized by evil and flawed by sin.

As we are drawn closer to God we become more aware of his character. The more we intuit his righteousness the more our lives come under his scrutiny and 'the righteous God trieth the very hearts and reins', exposing the secrets of our heart.

As I prayed and prepared myself for surgery by reading Brother Lawrence's *The Practice of the Presence of God* and Henry Drummond's *The Greatest Thing in the World* I was aware of my heart being laid bare before God. How I longed for a pure heart.

The 'true of heart' are not those who think themselves perfect but rather those who dare not raise their eyes, let alone their voices, to heaven and simply plead, 'Lord, have mercy.' Even though 'God is provoked every day' he will preserve the 'true of heart' for he is 'strong, and patient' (v. 12) and will forgive even the impure thoughts of our hearts.

Pray

Almighty God, unto whom all hearts be open, all desires known, and from whom no secrets are hid; Cleanse the thoughts of our hearts by the inspiration of thy Holy Spirit, that we may perfectly love thee, and worthily magnify thy holy Name; through Christ our Lord. Amen.

(Book of Common Prayer,
Collect for Purity, Holy Communion)

Psalm 9.1

I will give thanks unto thee, O Lord, with my whole heart:
I will speak of all thy marvellous works.

A truly grateful heart is rarely seen or heard. It goes against the grain of entitlement whereby people expect their rights to be delivered. It runs counter to the tenor of most conversations where complaint is the litany of the day.

We're more affected by this prevailing mood of dissatisfaction than we realize. If ever there were a sign of a faith-inspired change of heart it is the expression of gratitude. Thankfulness reveals a heart in which the donor rather than the recipient lies at the centre of the world. It is the polar opposite of entitlement. Yet paradoxically in the act of giving the donor makes the recipient his or her centre!

Yet you can never tell anyone to say 'Thank you', for the moment you do the words are emptied. Thanksgiving is necessarily a voluntary gesture of the heart. That is why, maybe, there is no explicit 'thanksgiving' in the Lord's Prayer.

If we could print out all the prayers we had ever thought or uttered I wonder what the proportion would be of petition to thanksgiving. In the Gospels ten lepers asked Jesus to heal them. Only one returned to say 'Thank you'. It's probably still about ten to one. I hereby resolve to balance the ratio.

Pray

Almighty God, Father of all mercies, we thine unworthy servants do give thee most humble and hearty thanks for all thy goodness and loving-kindness to us, and to all men; We bless thee for our creation, preservation, and all the blessings of this life; but above all for thine inestimable love in the redemption of the world by our Lord Jesus Christ, for the means of grace, and for the hope of glory. And, we beseech thee, give us that due sense of all thy mercies, that our hearts may be unfeignedly thankful, and that we shew forth thy praise, not only with our lips, but in our lives; by giving up ourselves to thy service, and by walking before thee in holiness and righteousness all our days; through Jesus Christ our Lord, to whom with thee and the Holy Ghost be all honour and glory, world without end. Amen.

(Book of Common Prayer, 'A General Thanksgiving')

Psalm 10.3

For the ungodly hath made boast of his own heart's desire:
and speaketh good of the covetous, whom God abhorreth.

One of the deceits of our egocentric world is the belief that whatever you desire should be the goal of your life. We're encouraged to dig deep into our inner self and unearth our buried desires. The mantra is, 'You can be whatever you want to be', 'Believe in yourself' and 'Make your dreams come true'. It's so seductive. It is disturbing to see how much this culture has infected the hearts of people of faith. The media constantly parade before us the few who have made their dreams come true – for a while. But there's seldom any attempt to assess the quality of these dreams and desires. Ambition is rooted in just seeing what others have got and wanting this for yourself, whatever the cost to others.

This psalm exposes the flaw in the heart's desire of the egocentric or, as they are described here, 'the ungodly'. It is characterized by a lust at the expense of others, especially the poor. In the world of these psalms the link between one person's ambitions and another's exploitation was more obvious. In our own day the connection between our wealth and another's poverty is more complex and obscure. Yet contemplating the possibility of such a link is one way of testing the quality of our heart's desires. There is nothing wrong with ambition. It all depends on what you are aiming for. But any sense that our ambitions will be at the expense of the poor will expose the ungodly direction in which we wish to travel.

Pray

Lord,
purify my heart
to dream of your desires. Amen.

Psalm 10.6, 12, 14

For he hath said in his heart, Tush, I shall never be cast down:
there shall no harm happen unto me.

He hath said in his heart, Tush, God hath forgotten:
he hideth away his face, and he will never see it.

Wherefore should the wicked blaspheme God:
while he doth say in his heart, Tush, thou God carest not for it.

The telltale signs of turning away from God mount up. We all have moments or episodes of distancing God from our innermost life, and each time we find a way of rationalizing and keeping him at arm's length. Each presumes upon him in a different way.

The first is to presume upon the silence of God and imagine that because we hear nothing there will be no repercussions to our half-hearted faith.

The second is to presume on the invisibility of God and imagine that because he is not seen he does not see all and therefore 'will never see it'.

The third is to presume on the passive nature of God who absorbs pain and suffering, and to conclude wrongly that 'God carest not', that our wickedness does not matter.

Each of these reactions has an insidious effect on our faith. A time of crisis can wake us up to how we have presumed on God. As I faced up to my own future I had to weigh up what 'harm [might] happen unto me'. I reviewed my life in the light that God had sight of it all and then humbled myself again under the hand of God.

Pray

Lord,
show me the difference
between divine silence
and indifference. Amen.

Psalm 10.19, 20

Lord, thou hast heard the desire of the poor:
thou preparest their heart, and thine ear hearkeneth thereto;
To help the fatherless and poor unto their right:
that the man of the earth be no more exalted against them.

It's a conundrum. In the richest regions of the world there is the greatest scepticism about God; in the poorest parts of the earth the belief in God is strongest. You might have thought it would have been the other way around with the materially satisfied reassured by God's providence and those in poverty railing against injustice as proof positive of God's absence or indifference.

It could be that the poor are holding on to the notion of pie in the sky when they die as some cosmic compensation for their misfortune. But this verse makes me think that the faith of the poor is evidence that God does indeed hear their cry and is actually and already preparing their hearts (for what is yet to come).

You cannot read the Bible without registering between the eyes that there is a dynamic progression towards the liberation of the whole of Creation, epitomized here by God's commitment to liberate and 'to help the fatherless and poor unto their right'.

The days are numbered for those who oppress them. We should prepare our own heart in the light of how God is already preparing the hearts of the poor 'unto their right'.

Pray

Lord,
give me an ear
to hear
the desire of the poor;
grant to me a heart
to part
with dreams against your law. Amen.

Psalm 15.1, 2

———•◆•———

Lord, who shall dwell in thy tabernacle:
or who shall rest upon thy holy hill?
Even he, that leadeth an uncorrupt life:
and doeth the thing which is right,
and speaketh the truth from his heart.

To live in harmony with heaven belongs to those who do what
is right and speak truth from the heart. This is an impossible
standard for any with an inkling of self-knowledge! If we were
to speak the truth from our heart about ourselves we would
have to confess to falling short of this gold standard. An uncorrupt life. Doing right. Not lying. No betrayal. No slander.
Humility. Honouring the godly. Faithfulness even at your own
expense. Taking no advantage of those in your debt.

Although the psalms are full of assurances that God is slow
to anger and abounding in compassion, this particular psalm
is uncompromising about the ideal. Many hundreds of years
before Christ it is a portrait of Jesus.

It is good to meditate upon the whole of this psalm and with
each verse encourage yourself to go on an excursion into the
life of Jesus to find examples of these ideals.

Even as a boy he was at home in the Temple quizzing the
priests. (What a pity those questions are not recorded!) As in
Rudyard Kipling's poem 'If', he could keep company with all
manner of people without being swayed or corrupted. To friend
and foe alike he always spoke the truth, from the heart.
Throughout his trial he never resorted to lies, slander or recrim-
ination. The depth of his humility is plumbed when on the

cross he begs forgiveness for those driving out the last breath from his body with nails.

If anyone imagines what God would be like should he be found walking the face of the earth they would surely draw such a picture.

The degree to which we find his life attractive offers us a thermometer-reading on the state of our heart before God.

Pray

O God, who hast prepared for them that love thee such good things as pass man's understanding; Pour into our hearts such love toward thee, that we, loving thee above all things, may obtain thy promises, which exceed all that we can desire; through Jesus Christ our Lord. Amen.

(Book of Common Prayer,
Collect for the Sixth Sunday after Trinity)

Psalm 16.9, 10

I have set God always before me:
for he is on my right hand, therefore I shall not fall.
Wherefore my heart was glad, and my glory rejoiced:
my flesh also shall rest in hope.

A glad heart often shows in the face. As does a sad heart. In the days after my surgery I caught sight of myself in the mirror and could see the heaviness of my heart in the lines on my face. Our culture of make-up, grooming and touching up photographs blurs the connection between the inner life and outward appearance, between the spiritual and the physical, even the physiological.

This psalm envisages a glad heart showing in a person's aura ('my glory rejoiced') and in a positive physical demeanour ('my flesh also shall rest in hope'). The prerequisite is neither diet, exercise nor vitamins, important though all these things are, but a spiritual remedy: to 'set God always before me'.

I first saw this in Albert. He had been a miner. Then he became verger of the church from which he retired when Parkinson's disease made it impossible for him to do his duties. He and his wife May lived on a pittance and in a rented terrace house, yet their faces radiated a gladness generated in their hearts. They tithed their income and out of it gave me money to buy theology books. They prayed for me faithfully. In spite of the ravages of the disease Albert's whole demeanour blazed with a passion, so much so that this whole psalm could have been written by him, and about him: 'I have set God always before me.'

Pray

Lord,
I will set thee before me;
be thou my hope and my glory! Amen.

Psalm 17.3

—————•◦•—————

Thou hast proved and visited mine heart in the night-season;
thou hast tried me, and shalt find no wickedness in me:
for I am utterly purposed that my mouth shall not offend.

'The dark night of the soul' is as common to human existence as suffering itself be it physical, mental or emotional, for, to extend to all humanity the words Shakespeare put into Shylock's mouth, 'sufferance is the badge of all our tribe'. To be able to talk about the soul's dark night sounds so noble, as if one can recognize this as a staging post on the spiritual pilgrimage. The truth is that when you are in the midst of 'the night-season' it doesn't feel like that; it feels like hell. The last thing you are able to do is to locate this inner trauma in a positive scheme of things. You feel as though you are drowning with all your fears crashing over your head and suffocating the breath out of you. If only you could recognize it as an episode of spiritual growth there would be some mild sedative for your anxieties. But the night season of the soul makes you panic that the dawn never will come again.

Yet this psalm talks of God doing a visitation of the heart, our heart, in the night season. All I can say to that is that it must occur under some form of anaesthetic for it happens without the slightest awareness of the patient!

Yet just as we become aware of surgery after the event as the anaesthesia wears off, so it is only after the night season that we begin to realize that we have been through the soul's dark night; and that in that raw and uncontrolled state we have been known to and by God.

There will be some telltale sign of the change in our relationship with God. Here the evidence comes in our language: 'I am utterly purposed that my mouth shall not offend.' Not surprisingly. Because 'in the night-season' to our shame we can hear ourselves uttering obscenities, such is the darkness of the night.

Pray

Lord,
visit mine heart,
shew thy marvellous loving-kindness,
thou that art the Saviour of them
which put their trust in thee.
Keep me as the apple of an eye:
hide me under the shadow of thy wings.

(based on Psalm 17.3a, 7 and 8)

Psalm 19.8, 14, 15

———•◆•———

The statutes of the Lord are right, and rejoice the heart:
the commandment of the Lord is pure,
and giveth light unto the eyes.

Let the words of my mouth, and the meditation of my heart:
be alway acceptable in thy sight,
O Lord: my strength, and my redeemer.

The West looks to the East for the art of meditation. There's an impatience about our way of life that militates against the leisure of meditating. There's also a way of thinking that deals in abstract concepts and lacks the concrete images which are often the first focus of meditation. For example, beginning with the abstract concept 'Love' can lead you down a different path from starting with a picture of a long-lost child ending up in the arms of his wronged and weeping father.

This psalm holds before us a picture of God seeing our heart at work. Here in this psalm meditation is not about emptying your mind, but about filling it with particular pictures of God. The heavens demonstrate his handiwork; night and day declare his craftsmanship; the sun that he has made rises like a bridegroom from his bed, like a giant joyfully running a race.

These images enlarge our vision of God by stirring the imagination, but only if we attend to them in a leisurely way. We can skate over them swiftly and be unaffected. Or we can savour them and then discover that they are 'more to be desired than gold' and 'sweeter also than honey, and the honey-comb' (v. 10).

Leisurely meditation on God's Creation and his laws can 'convert the soul' (v. 7) and keep you from sin. The advantage of convalescence is to have the time although not always the mental energy to meditate on God.

Yet God is not simply the object of our meditation; he is in the audience, a spectator, watching the theatre of our thoughts from the balcony of heaven. This is a picture worthy of meditation.

Meditation

Meditate on the curtain rising before God on the current scene of your life.

Psalm 20.1, 4

The Lord hear thee in the day of trouble:
the Name of the God of Jacob defend thee;

Grant thee thy heart's desire:
and fulfil all thy mind.

It is a commentary on our human condition that although occasionally it is joy that propels us into the arms of God, more often than not it is a crisis that drives us to our knees in prayer. It is only when our self-sufficiency is drained and we come to the end of our self that we create space for others and for God.

This is the silver lining to the darkest cloud. The day of trouble becomes the day of defence.

This psalm is a prayer for a friend in trouble, that the Lord would grant him his 'heart's desire'. Presumably his mind and heart are set on being delivered out of his troubles. The prayer assumes that this accords with the will of God.

Each act of deliverance is like a distant wave that gathers in momentum and size with the incoming tide and crashes on to the shore, wave after wave drenching the beach until the tide turns and drains the debris from the shore. Deliverance and rescue in the psalms, and throughout the Bible, is a story that is repeated with the promise of a grand climax, when on another shore there will be no more pain, dying, crying or grieving.

Troubles keep coming in life. There are times when we may think that God owes us for our commitment, so that when troubles come, we feel let down, as if God has not kept his side of the bargain.

But Scripture shows a path of endurance and deliverance.

To be delivered once – as these prayers make clear – does not immunize you from further episodes of trouble. They are a foretaste of the grand deliverance. Be equally wary of those who say that our existence is a perpetual Good Friday and of those who pretend that it will be a constant Easter Sunday. We move back and forwards, to and from endurance and deliverance. Then one day . . . !

Pray this ancient prayer

Maranatha,
come, Lord, come!
    (see 1 Corinthians 16.22 and Revelation 22.20)

Psalm 21.2, 3

Thou hast given him his heart's desire:
and hast not denied him the request of his lips.
For thou shalt prevent him with the blessings of goodness:
and shalt set a crown of pure gold upon his head.

The subject of this psalm is the King. Those called to preside over and lead a nation bear an awesome responsibility before both the people and God. It is good that we should pray for them. Because 'absolute power corrupts absolutely', it is important not just to have checks and balances within the system but to have rulers who are humbled by believing that they are answerable to God. The decisions of those with power affect the futures of us all. Here, 'the King putteth his trust in the Lord: and in the mercy of the most Highest he shall not miscarry' (v. 7). It's a picture of a monarch resplendent at his coronation, yet humbly kneeling at the feet of the God of mercy.

This humility is captured by the Prayer Book in the Accession Service in the penultimate prayer:

We beseech thee to have compassion upon our infirmities;
and those things, which for our unworthiness we dare not,
and for our blindness we cannot ask, vouchsafe to give us,
for the worthiness of thy Son Jesus Christ our Lord.

To such a mercy-seeking servant God responds with grace, or as the psalm says: 'For thou shalt prevent him with the blessings of goodness . . .' which means that even before the heart has made its request God has begun to strew his path with blessings.

Pray

Pray, therefore, for Parliament under the Crown and for ourselves that we might know 'the blessings of goodness' and the mercy of God, which is that 'gentle dew from heaven'.

Psalm 22.14

I am poured out like water, and all my bones are out of joint:
my heart also in the midst of my body is even like melting wax.

Recovering from heart surgery I could not find a more vivid expression to describe my aching body and soul. Anaesthesia, sedation and painkillers were God's gift to numb the physical discomfort; but 'poured out', 'out of joint' and 'melting wax' capture the emotional and spiritual discomfort.

The day after I got home and was tasting a bowl of soup in the kitchen with Sarah, my wife, I found the tears streaming down my face with no desire either to staunch them or contain the shuddering sob. It was not catastrophe, but catharsis. Much had led up to this moment, and equally, much was flowing out from it.

My only hesitation in appropriating this verse to describe my own experience is the knowledge that Jesus drew heavily on this psalm to interpret his crucifixion and death.

In Rogier van der Weyden's painting *Descent from the Cross* the contour of Mary, the mourning mother, mirrors exactly the shape of the body of her beloved son, Jesus, being taken down from the cross. It's as if the grieving mother is telling the world how exactly she feels the pain of her child. Yet there's another possible interpretation. Maybe it tells us that the bent body of Jesus aches symmetrically with the bitter bereavement of his own mother.

Jesus doubly bereaved, of God his heavenly Father and Mary his earthly mother. One of us 'from the womb to the tomb'. Here is 'a man of sorrows' and 'acquainted with grief' (Isaiah 53.3 KJV).

Therefore, in him we have one who knows us and knows what it means to be 'poured out like water', to have his 'bones out of joint' and for his heart to feel 'like melting wax'. As surely as he felt the sorrow of his mother's soul he feels the melting of our own heart.

Pray

Lord,
pour the molten wax
of my heart
into the mould
of thy cross. Amen.

Psalm 24.1, 3, 4

The earth is the Lord's, and all that therein is:
the compass of the world, and they that dwell therein.

Who shall ascend into the hill of the Lord:
or who shall rise up in his holy place?
Even he that hath clean hands, and a pure heart:
and that hath not lift up his mind unto vanity,
nor sworn to deceive his neighbour.

God is the Lord of earth and heaven. The Lord's Prayer is for the fusion of the two. Asking for God's will to be done in earth as it is done in heaven is a prayer for the earthing of heaven. The rebellion in the Garden of Eden drove a wedge between the two realms. The history of God's salvation tells of how God reconciles the two.

It does not take much evidence to demonstrate that heaven and earth are not at one. Although 'the earth is the Lord's, and all that therein is', it is dominated by systems and people out of tune with the ethos and ethics of the Creator.

Our hands are soiled and 'the soil is bare now' for, as G. M. Hopkins sketched in his poem 'God's Grandeur',

> . . . all is seared with trade; bleared, smeared with toil;
> And wears man's smudge and shares man's smell.

Yet in spite of this pessimistic criticism of our treatment of Creation the poet traces hope: 'And for all this, nature is never spent.' Why?

Because the Holy Ghost over the bent
World broods with warm breast and with ah!
   bright wings.

And who shall inherit this new earth and new heaven? According to Jesus, the meek, described here as those with 'clean hands, and a pure heart: and that hath not lift up his mind unto vanity, nor sworn to deceive his neighbour'.

The purity of our heart shows in our relationship not just with the Creator but with his creatures and all Creation.

Pray

Thy will be done, in earth as it is in heaven.

(Book of Common Prayer, from the Lord's Prayer)

Psalm 25.1, 16, 17

Unto thee, O Lord, will I lift up my soul;
my God, I have put my trust in thee:
O let me not be confounded,
neither let mine enemies triumph over me.

The sorrows of my heart are enlarged:
O bring thou me out of my troubles.
Look upon my adversity and misery:
and forgive me all my sin.

There is some adversity, though not all, that we bring on ourselves. We need to be cautious about this, because the first reaction we have to calamities is to imagine that God must be punishing us for something we have done. As Jesus made clear of a man born blind, that is not how God operates in his world. Nevertheless, there are consequences to our actions and sometimes we say or do what we know to be wrong and experience dire results. However much we may try to rationalize and excuse our behaviour we are left with a conscience that is seared and restless, and 'the sorrows of [our] heart are enlarged'.

This inner turmoil makes us miserable. We can harbour it for years and take into middle age some wrong unresolved from our younger years. In the end the self-justification brings no peace. We have no hope but to turn to God and plead:

O remember not the sins and offences of my youth: but according to thy mercy think thou upon me, O Lord, for thy goodness.

> Gracious and righteous is the Lord: therefore will he teach
> sinners in the way. (Psalm 25.6–7)

It is God's heart's desire to lift the large sorrows of our heart,
even those we load upon ourselves. He is good and gracious
and comes running, like the Good Father to the Prodigal Son,
who could echo these words:

> Turn thee unto me, and have mercy upon me: for I am
> desolate, and in misery. (Psalm 25.15)

It is through God's forgiveness that our 'soul shall dwell at ease'
(v. 12). The redeemability of offenders, however old our years
and our sins, lies at the heart of God's mission.

Pray

Lord,
forgive me all my sin
and my soul
shall dwell at ease. Amen.

Psalm 26.1, 2

Be thou my Judge, O Lord, for I have walked innocently:
my trust hath been also in the Lord, therefore shall I not fall.
Examine me, O Lord, and prove me:
try out my reins and my heart.

Enough of sin! Here is the portrait of a blameless believer, someone who in all honesty before God cannot point to any wilful act of disobedience. And yet. Even with a conscience clear before God this plaintiff appears to plead with the Judge of all to examine him forensically: 'Prove me: try out my reins and my heart.' Usually we pray this sort of prayer and call upon God as the merciful Judge when seeking his compassion and forgiveness. Seldom do we bring ourselves before the bar of heaven when satisfied with the performance of our duties.

But like an athlete who's come first and a musician who's given a virtuoso performance, who continue to submit to the coach and the maestro, so too faithful pilgrims are not content to rest on their laurels. They press on to perfection.

In the relationship with God the child of God does not settle for just doing the right thing. There is more to this relationship than moral duty. The clue is in the verse that follows: 'For thy loving-kindness is ever before mine eyes.' One of the snares of religion is the lapse into dutiful ritual. Being taken away forcibly from my religious duties has given me the leisure to examine my own heart, to look beyond duty and to feel again the 'Love that will not let me go'.

Love is the baring of one heart to the other. As God, out of love, discloses to us his own heart through Creation, through Christ Jesus and the cross, so in turn we open our heart to him saying, 'Try out my reins and my heart.'

Pray

Lord,
thy love my heart constrains;
try out my reins
that I might live for thee
who died and rose for me. Amen.

Psalm 27.9

My heart hath talked of thee, Seek ye my face:
Thy face, Lord, will I seek.

In St Paul's famous essay on love he writes about how one day we will see God face to face but for now we see 'through a glass, darkly' (1 Corinthians 13.12 KJV). It's a poetic phrase conveying the original Greek which literally says that we see through a glass not darkly but 'in an enigma'. In our desire to know God fully, as fully as we are known by him, we are limited by our earthly existence. We do not, as it were, have the language of heaven to speak of God: all that we have are enigmas, parables, pictures, similes, allegories and metaphors. That is why theology, even as 'Queen of the Sciences', is such an inexact one.

The metaphor before us is typically enigmatic. 'Thy face, Lord, will I seek.' But no one except the Son has seen God. And when God revealed himself through the Son, his biographers, the Gospel writers, gave no details of his physical appearance. We have no idea of the human face of God in spite of icons, shrouds, mosaics and paintings. They, like language, are beautiful but enigmatic.

Nevertheless, the force of this verse lies in the longing it expresses: 'My heart hath talked of thee . . .' This yearning is the best mode for the heart to be in.

Even though for us seeing God face to face belongs to the next chapter of life, the metaphor assumes the face of God is already turned in our direction. The unseen face of God, that our heart desires to see, is already fixed with grace upon our own. So, as our heart talks of its desire to see God, we set

ourselves before his face and under the ancient blessing of
Aaron:

> The LORD bless thee, and keep thee: The LORD make his
> face shine upon thee, and be gracious unto thee: The LORD
> lift up his countenance upon thee, and give thee peace.
> (Numbers 6.24–26 KJV)

Then one day, as Jesus prophesied, there will be no more need
for parables – or enigmas. We shall see as we are seen.

Pray

Pray the blessing of Aaron, putting 'me' in place of 'thee'.

Psalm 27.15, 16

I should utterly have fainted:
but that I believe verily to see the goodness of
the Lord in the land of the living.
O tarry thou the Lord's leisure:
be strong, and he shall comfort thine heart;
and put thou thy trust in the Lord.

With these words I began to come to terms with the news that
I was to have major heart surgery. All of us have our own stories
of confronting something we dread, and then feeling faint.
Ever since doing biology at school I had been squeamish and
nervous about the inner workings of the body. I chide myself
for being so pathetic! But when all is stripped away that is what
I am, which I confessed to my understanding consultants and
nurses – and to God. Often!

When first I read these words they spoke to my heart as if
to say that God both knew this and understood. I started to
laugh. Here in the Book of Common Prayer, in the Psalms – 'I
should utterly have fainted' – God put his finger on my pulse
and knew me. It happens from time to time that you read
something and sense it was written for you. It comes off the
page with a nudge and a wink. But the words that lingered in
my heart were: 'O tarry thou the Lord's leisure.'

The thought of God at leisure now inviting me to tune my
life to his instrument and to a slower rhythm relieved the ten-
sion within me. It enabled me to surrender myself into the
hands of the medical team and to whatever God purposed for
me. By nature I am an activist. I find fulfilment working with

a team to achieve things together. But here I was, in Vanstone's phrase from *The Stature of Waiting*, moving from the active to the passive. This is not to be resisted or resented for, as Vanstone showed, at the Passion of our Lord he went from activity to passivity, from being the subject of all the verbs to becoming the object. In his Passion he fulfilled God's purpose as much as when he was in control of the action.

And with this did the Lord comfort my heart.

Pray

Lord,
lead me leisurely
in thy way. Amen.

Psalm 28.8

The Lord is my strength, and my shield;
my heart hath trusted in him, and I am helped:
therefore my heart danceth for joy,
and in my song will I praise him.

Through all his trials and tribulations St Paul urged others to discover with him that God's strength is made perfect in human weakness, and that his grace is always sufficient. These are discoveries we do not always wish to make! They involve us in situations where we feel vulnerable. Asked if we would like to venture forth on such a spiritual assault course most of us would decline in favour of the security of the familiar. Yet throughout the five decades when I have consciously sought to follow Jesus I have noticed a pattern.

The journey has been marked by a series of milestones, seed-size realizations of God's purposes. At unpredictable moments I have been brought to a point of deeper self-knowledge and called to trust more than before. I use the passive mode deliberately for I have hardly ever sought these. These episodes have often been disorientating and at the time seldom held out the promise of enlightenment.

Even the reaching out to God from the depths has not always been the first thought of my heart. But sometimes we are like the 'horse and mule, which have no understanding' who 'must be held with bit and bridle' (see Psalm 32.10). As we feel the constraint of circumstances eventually we yield the reins of our heart to the invisible hand of God.

More often than not and after a struggle it felt his hand was 'heavy upon me day and night' (Psalm 32.4). Then through sheer exhaustion under the weight of it all my heart went into reflex and just trusted in God for the future.

The one discovery I have made is that any desire to dance was in measure equal to the length of the struggle.

But it is on looking back I can say with this psalm that I have been helped. And only, it seems, can I say so in retrospect.

Reflection

With the verse above consider one episode when you feel God may have helped you. Do not let go of this memory until your heart has spoken.

Psalm 31.27

Be strong, and he shall establish your heart:
all ye that put your trust in the Lord.

Jesus, of all people, knew the human heart. He knew how fickle the heart could be. He could see what flowed from it and knew what it was capable of, both good and bad. I don't think any human being would dissent from that assessment. The heart is like a rudderless boat that turns with every current and breeze. Those who put their trust in God anchor their hearts in him. The promise of this psalm is that God 'shall establish your heart'. This is a vital promise.

After the resurrection and before his Ascension Jesus appeared to his disciples. He breathed over them saying, 'Receive the Holy Spirit.' These traumatized followers knew just how feeble their hearts had been during the dark days of his trial and crucifixion. I've often wondered whether they felt his breath, and, if they did, whether they consciously breathed it in and inhaled the Holy Spirit.

Following my operation I was encouraged to do breathing exercises. Sometimes I did them imagining Jesus breathing over me saying, 'Receive the Holy Spirit.' As I breathed in as deeply as I could it became a spiritual exercise of taking to my heart all the health and strength that Jesus has to offer.

Sometimes hymns came to mind:

> Breathe on me, breath of God,
> Fill me with life anew,
> That I might love what thou dost love,
> And do what thou wouldst do.

Breathe on me, breath of God,
Until my heart is pure,
Until with thee I will one will,
To do and to endure.
(E. Hatch, 1835–89)

With such imaginative exercises we open not just our mind but our body to God so that he might establish our heart and give us strength.

Pray

(with your breathing)

Receive the Holy Spirit.

Psalm 32.12

Be glad, O ye righteous, and rejoice in the Lord:
and be joyful, all ye that are true of heart.

This psalm with its final verse offers hope to us all because the 'true of heart' at the end of the song are none other than the unrighteous at the beginning! When we become aware of the call of God to commit our life or to give ourselves more wholeheartedly we can hold back on the grounds that we are simply not good enough. Conscious of our own failings we feel that to aspire to such greater commitment is beyond our grasp.

The transformation comes when we realize that God will take us where we are. 'I said, I will confess my sins unto the Lord' (v. 6).

Trueness of heart is not an achievement but a gift that comes with the response of God to our confession. It is a blessing bestowed on us when God declares us forgiven. The 'godly' are not the self-righteously good but those who make their prayer to God honestly out of their sense of unworthiness. They are those who treat him as a place to hide from all accusers, including the self, often the most critical, especially in times of crisis.

In hospital and during my recovery the longing for that joy was constantly depressed by a preoccupation with myself – the progress I was or was not making and the state of my heart, physical and spiritual. It was only naked acknowledgement of this self-absorbed condition that unlocked the door and allowed grace to medicate my heart, both of them.

Pray

Lord, have mercy upon me,
make true my heart
and glad in thee. Amen.

Psalm 33.11, 14, 20

The counsel of the Lord shall endure for ever:
and the thoughts of his heart from generation to generation.

He fashioneth all the hearts of them:
and understandeth all their works.

For our heart shall rejoice in him:
because we have hoped in his holy Name.

The heart of God. This is holy ground. Who dares speak of it? Who dares to tread there?

This psalm comes to a crescendo with a psalm of praise to the heart of God. His word is true, his works are faithful, he loves justice, he's made the earth full of goodness and oceans full of treasure. These are just some of the signs of the providence that flows from the heart of God.

The artistic Creator has also fashioned the hearts of those he's made in his own image. Thus from one heart to another, the divine to the human, he has given us the capacity to hear his word, understand his works, discern and do what is just and enjoy the fruits of the earth and the sea. So, in this song, the heart of God speaks to the heart of humanity through Creation and conscience. In such communion the human heart finds joy.

There are many people whose hearts turn cold at the thought of church but who come alive spiritually in a garden or a forest, or walking the wolds, the moors and the dales. Equally there are many whose hearts are turned against the Church because of abuse and who out of a passion for justice champion the cause of the poor, the powerless and the prisoner. Lest those of us in the Church discount them we need to confess the complicity of the Church in the neglect of both God's Creation and injustice.

Yet the point here is that the human heart was fashioned by God's heart to delight in his Creation and discern and do what is just. Whenever and wherever the human heart is so alive we should celebrate.

We of the Church have much to learn about God's heart, about conscience and Creation, about discerning and delighting, from those human hearts who act justly and tread the earth humbly. Our calling is to learn from them and then in friendship to trace back from their intuition to discover '[the] holy Name' of him in whom we all 'live and move and have our being' (Acts 17.28).

Consider one feature of Creation and one issue of conscience.

Pray

Lord,
fashion my heart
to love what you have made
to do what is right
and to rejoice in your goodness. Amen.

Psalm 34.1, 18

I will alway give thanks unto the Lord:
his praise shall ever be in my mouth.

The Lord is nigh unto them that are of a contrite heart:
and will save such as be of an humble spirit.

Contrition comes in many guises. A bogus one is betrayed by the little word 'if', for example, 'I'm sorry if you feel so upset.' This apology is qualified. It transfers responsibility away from the culprit and on to the victim. Instead of taking the weight of the blame the apologizer shifts the blame on to the victim for being so distressed. There's a world of difference between 'I'm sorry if I've upset you' and 'I'm sorry that I've upset you.' The next time the word 'sorry' is on your lips it's worth pausing to ask what stops you from turning the 'if' into a 'that'.

This psalm gives signs of the contrite heart. The two are humility and thanksgiving.

The truly contrite person is humble before the aggrieved. It is pride that refuses to acknowledge failure and culpability; it is pride that goes the extra mile and then some more to find remote reasons for our action; it is pride that resists allowing the offended to occupy moral ground higher than our own. Humility in the offender creates room for the crushed to unfold and to fill the space violated by the offence and even to contemplate the thought of the relationship being restored.

With humility comes also thanksgiving. The truly contrite heart tastes and sees how gracious the Lord is. Gratitude for that experience encourages you to believe further that whereas 'lions do lack, and suffer hunger: but they who seek the Lord shall want no manner of thing that is good' (v. 10). The thankful heart is a recipient of providence, from the fruits of Creation to the bonds of compassion.

Pray

Holding out both hands, let God place in one the globe and in the other the cross.

Give thanks for both.

Psalm 35.20, 25

Their communing is not for peace:
but they imagine deceitful words against them that are
quiet in the land.

Let them not say in their hearts, There, there, so would we have it:
neither let them say, We have devoured him.

Civilized and liberal societies that over the centuries have
tamed the wilder elements of humanity find the concepts of
original sin and evil either unfamiliar or uncomfortable. But,
as Golding's *Lord of the Flies* showed, these realities lurk under-
neath the surface in very shallow waters. Civilization is the
result of people communing with their hearts and imagining
a world in which people love their neighbour as themselves.
And peace comes to the heart, the home, the street and the city
in differing degrees.

Yet this sense of civil security can be very suddenly shattered
if a determined group of wilful provocateurs seek to undermine
it. I write this in the week that hooligans are vandalizing our
cities.

Whatever the social and economic dimensions to this disturbance are, there are also moral and spiritual ones too. The heart
is not neutral. It can aspire to good or ill. It is the seat of the will.
Not every heart communes 'for peace' – sadly some imagine
the ruination of the 'quiet in the land'.

Being ill and laid up detaches you from the world and renders
you an observer of human nature. An accurate assessment of
our condition recognizes, as did Jesus, 'it is from within, from
the human heart that evil intentions come'. This is not a counsel

of despair for, as the psalms show, the heart can be converted for good.

But they also show that there are supernatural forces at work in the world which are the enemies of peace. These hostile powers, which Jesus himself encountered, inhabit the spiritual world, and find fertile soil in the unconverted heart. It is a toxic mix.

Pray

Give peace in our time, O Lord.

Because there is none other that fighteth for us, but only thou, O God.

O God, make clean our hearts within us.

> (Book of Common Prayer,
> from Morning and Evening Prayer)

Psalm 36.1, 10

My heart sheweth me the wickedness of the ungodly:
that there is no fear of God before his eyes.

O continue forth thy loving-kindness unto them that know thee:
and thy righteousness unto them that are true of heart.

Read the whole of this psalm for a portrait of the unconverted heart that does not 'abhor any thing that is evil' (v. 4). The root problem is that 'there is no fear of God before his eyes'.

In the chapel at Bishop's Lodge where we live and work there's a sculpture over the Lord's Table of Jesus bent over the city weeping, 'If only you knew the things that make for peace' (see Luke 19.41–42). For centuries the Church has built up the experience of community across the country. It continues to play a unique role in regeneration. It recognizes the importance of the environment, the economy and education to the well-being of our neighbourhoods, and it holds out for another vital dimension: spiritual regeneration. The Christian faith is a converting religion. It believes in transformation. The encounter with God through the Spirit of Jesus Christ changes the heart. The evidence of this shows in a new attitude to God, to others and to yourself. The greatest blight I have seen in areas of deprivation and among prisoners is low self-esteem and low aspiration.

These things are the enemies of regeneration. Time and again I have witnessed the power of the antidote which comes when, through a caring community, a person becomes aware of God's 'loving-kindness' for him or her personally. This ultimately is what makes for peace in the human heart and in our communities. This experience sensitizes the conscience and stirs the imagination to think of and care for others. The feeling that God loves you moves you to value yourself and to find out God's purpose for your life. When this yeast leavens the loaf in more and more lives it has a civilizing impact on the whole community. This is a distinctive contribution that faith makes for peace. You can restore the fabric of a neighbourhood but unless people care for each other the word 'community' is misplaced.

Meditate

Picture Jesus standing on the edge of where you live.
See the tears in his eyes.
Hear the words, 'If only you knew what makes for peace.'
What do you think might distress him about your
  neighbourhood?

Psalm 37.4, 7, 32

Delight thou in the Lord:
and he shall give thee thy heart's desire.

Hold thee still in the Lord, and abide patiently upon him:
but grieve not thyself at him, whose way doth prosper,
against the man that doeth after evil counsels.

The law of his God is in his heart:
and his goings shall not slide.

The promise of God to give us our heart's desires is conditional. When our heart is in tune with God's heart and hence our will with his will then, as Jesus said, 'Ask for whatever you wish, and it will be done for you' (John 15.7 NRSV). The secret is to stay close to him: 'Hold thee still in the Lord.'

But this abiding in him patiently is far from easy for there are many distractions for the heart, not least the sight of others who seem to succeed without any regard for God at all. The immoral and the unjust, the selfish and the arrogant, seem to prosper with impunity. Not only does that strike most of us as unfair, it can also make us doubt the wisdom of our commitment to act justly, love mercy and walk humbly with God (see Micah 6.8). What this psalm does is to act like a camera that tracks back and offers a wider angle on the panorama of human destiny. Whatever success the ungodly may now enjoy there will be a day of reckoning for us all, including them.

One day, again as Jesus promised 'the meek-spirited shall possess the earth' (v. 11; cf. Matthew 5.5) and the mean-spirited shall be deprived of all that they have exploited. I know that this sense of spiritual accountability is rare in today's world, but it is no less true because it is ignored.

As the psalm says, 'A small thing that the righteous hath: is better than great riches of the ungodly'(v. 16). The 'God of small things' can make our heart delight in such meek measures. Again, one of the blessings of being laid up lies in the scaling down of one's expectations and in an ever greater appreciation for the ever smaller things in life.

Pray

Lord,
in thee
hold me
still
to do thy will
contentedly. Amen.

Psalm 38.8, 10

I am feeble, and sore smitten:
I have roared for the very disquietness of my heart.

My heart panteth, my strength hath failed me:
and the sight of mine eyes is gone from me.

The success of those who trample on others with no regard for God or any moral principles can be very confusing for those of us who try to live our life by faith. It's not unusual for us to make a costly decision in favour of doing what we believe to be right before God and then find ourselves knocked backwards. It's as if we think that, having done God a favour, he should now reward us for our good deed. These experiences can tempt us to blow cold about our commitment, and soon we begin to compromise on our ideals. Soon the heart that has found peace with God finds its strength failing.

'The disquietness of my heart' can begin to show in physical symptoms that can affect the skin, the bones and the heart. Some psychosomatic illness can issue from a disorientated inner life. And even when we suspect this we block our ears and refuse to bring our situation candidly before God. We seem weighed down by an invisible heaviness. The only way for it to lift is to 'confess my wickedness: and be sorry for my sin' (v. 18).

Of course, most physical illnesses have physical causes, but a heart that is troubled by disobedience to God can show not only in the face but in a person's whole demeanour. This, confessed, meets only with the mercy of God.

Pray

Try me, O God, and seek the ground of my heart: prove me, and examine my thoughts. Look well if there be any wickedness in me: and lead me in the way everlasting.

(Psalm 139.23–24)

Psalm 39.1, 4, 5

I said, I will take heed to my ways:
that I offend not in my tongue.

My heart was hot within me, and while I was thus musing
the fire kindled:
and at the last I spake with my tongue;
Lord, let me know mine end, and the number of my days:
that I may be certified how long I have to live.

The tongue and heart, two organs at the centre of life. As this
psalm shows, what goes on in the metaphorical heart eventually comes out through the tongue literally. Bridling the tongue
and muzzling the mouth especially when faced with those who
have it in for you seems an impossible way of controlling your
emotions. Eventually there's an explosion. Instead of trying the
wilful biting of the lip in the face of provocation the psalm
proposes a prayer: 'Lord, let me know mine end, and the number
of my days.' It is when we realize how fleeting life is that we
make the better decisions. 'Life's too short . . .' for so much of
the aggression to which the human heart is disposed. Our life
span especially compared with eternity is like a shadow. Such
knowledge should turn us to God again with 'truly my hope
is even in thee' (v. 8). It is this that puts a zip on our lip or, as
it says more eloquently here, 'I became dumb, and opened not
my mouth: for it was thy doing' (v. 10).

I've been struck in my convalescence by the inverse pro-
portions of frustration and energy – the heart has certainly
got hotter more often and more quickly but the strength to

give vent has dipped to a new low. Illness has brought new perspectives. It makes you aware of limitations of both energy and time. Feeling too weak to rise to some indignation feels at first like a defeat. But there's blessing to be had in saving your breath. Both the spiritual and physical hearts benefit. Moreover, numbering your days can help humble the heart and tether the tongue.

Pray

Let me know mine end, and the number of my days.

Psalm 40.10, 12, 15

In the volume of the book it is written of me,
that I should fulfil thy will, O my God:
I am content to do it; yea, thy law is within my heart.

I have not hid thy righteousness within my heart:
my talk hath been of thy truth, and of thy salvation.

For innumerable troubles are come about me;
my sins have taken such hold upon me
that I am not able to look up:
yea, they are more in number than the hairs of my head,
and my heart hath failed me.

To be content to do only the will of God is how God originally fashioned the heart to be. With the gift of freedom came also the risk that the human heart might chase after other desires. These psalms testify to the vagaries of the heart, but they also capture the contentment of the heart when the will wills the will of God.

Here we find yet more signs of the union between the human heart and the heart of God. 'Thy law is within my heart.' God's law is found in the moral principles of the Ten Commandments.

'I have not hid thy righteousness within my heart.' God's passion for what is right is to be found in our action for justice.

'My talk hath been of thy truth.' The words that flow from our heart reveal our commitment to what is true.

Keeping God's law, acting justly, telling the truth, these are the signs of a heart at one with God. The one person who manifested all three was Jesus, who was so perfectly in tune with God that he was able to say, 'Whoever has seen me has seen the Father' (John 14.9 NRSV); 'The Father and I are one' (John 10.30 NRSV). If all these concepts of truth, justice and law are too skeletal or too abstract, they take on flesh with the birth of Jesus. All that you would expect to see in the heart of God you find in the person of Jesus. A heart that is drawn to him is a heart tuning itself to the silent music of God's Creation. Therein lies the contented heart.

Meditate

'Sir, we would see Jesus.' (John 12.21 KJV)

Postscript

Write your name in this book as a sign of your name being written by God in the volume that records all those who seek to do his will.

Psalm 41.1, 6

Blessed is he that considereth the poor and needy:
the Lord shall deliver him in the time of trouble.

And if [mine enemy] come to see me, he speaketh vanity:
and his heart conceiveth falsehood within himself,
and when he cometh forth he telleth it.

Poverty is evidence of a world out of kilter with its Creator. Anyone acting to relieve it finds a following wind of God's favour.

The causes of poverty are the enemies of God. In a world of great complexity it is not always easy to identify them, nor is it simple to find the remedies. The causes range from trading tariffs to the changing climate, from war to corruption and exploitation. Those with the power to make a difference on behalf of the poor, who are relatively powerless to help themselves, bear a greater responsibility before God.

The temptation to all of us who have a vested interest in maintaining the status quo, which favours the prosperous, is to respond with rhetoric or deny the truth of the analysis. Considering the poor will win you God's favour, but risks making you many enemies. When William Wilberforce sought with others to abolish the slave trade he was told that such a move would ruin the empire. Such was the 'vanity' and 'falsehood' of his opponents' arguments and hearts.

But the blessing to be found in considering the poor leads to an unexpected discovery, rather like digging for shells and finding pearls. It is in the poor that we come face to face with

God. Jesus told us that we would meet him in the least, the last and the lost. We might not realize it at first but he promised one day we would come to see that it was when visiting a prisoner or feeding a hungry tramp or comforting the destitute that we came nearest to him.

This adds new possibilities for those seeking after faith who reach out and say, 'If you are there, God, please show yourself to me.'

Meditate

It is not difficult through papers, magazines and even junk mail to find a picture of the poor. Hold it before you in prayer until you see him.

Psalm 44.19, 20, 21

Our heart is not turned back:
neither our steps gone out of thy way;
No, not when thou hast smitten us into the place of dragons:
and covered us with the shadow of death.
If we have forgotten the Name of our God,
and holden up our hands to any strange god:
shall not God search it out?
for he knoweth the very secrets of the heart.

Nothing is hidden from God. To him we are an open book. He knows the biography of each of us. Such knowledge is both disturbing and reassuring. The heart is in a marketplace where different desirables compete for our attention. Even when we have made our choice we can be dogged with second thoughts and doubt the decision we have made. All sorts of 'strange gods' can swan around our imagination and bring us down, so low that we feel ground into the dust. All those who have put their trust in God know something of this struggle. It is why at the service of baptism we are warned of the battle with the world, the flesh and the devil.

In this psalm the experience of being 'covered with the shadow of death' brings to a head this struggle in 'the place of dragons' (v. 20). In the end there are only two ways, the way of death and the way of life. It is salutary how the shadow of death brings this division into sharper focus, so much so that it becomes yet another well-disguised blessing.

I found the prospect of dying brought a fresh simplicity to my life and faith. Suddenly the questions and contradictions disappeared and the compound doubts dissolved like a soluble aspirin in water. The light behind death's shadow lit up the simple choice for my heart – to turn back or to trust. And in my secret heart God heard my prayer: 'Arise, and help us: and deliver us for thy mercy's sake' (v. 26).

Make this your prayer

Arise, and help me:
deliver me for the sake of thy mercy. Amen.

Psalm 45.1

My heart is inditing of a good matter:
I speak of the things which I have made unto the King.

Because the heart is the seat of the will it has the authority to direct the imagination. This psalm is a paean of praise to the king. To a cynical age as ours it sounds somewhat sycophantic! You are, in our time, unlikely to hear such praise for our leaders and those in authority. But the composer of this song admires the king for three explicit reasons.

'Good luck have thou with thine honour: ride on, because of the word of truth, of meekness, and righteousness' (v. 5a). God had blessed the king with three virtues of leadership – truth, humility and justice.

One of the blessings of convalescing is to have time on your hands. Suddenly we have all the time in the world! I found I had more time to pray, although I confess the prayers were like a box of frogs, jumping around in small hops and in all directions. Yet in spite of the erratic leaps my heart turned to pray for those in authority – the Queen, the future King, the Prime Minister. The city riots, the economic uncertainty, the international instability, the environmental threats all require the leadership of wisdom and in particular these three virtues of truth, humility and justice. It sounds quaint to pray that our leaders should be blessed with 'good luck' (v. 5a). Here it means good fortune and victory over the enemy.

Pray

As both the Bible and Prayer Book bid us:

> O God,
> to those in authority
> grant truth, humility and justice,
> and good luck in the name of the Lord. Amen.

Psalm 49.3, 4

My mouth shall speak of wisdom:
and my heart shall muse of understanding.
I will incline mine ear to the parable:
and shew my dark speech upon the harp.

The heart is the seat of the will. It is also the mat for meditation where we muse imaginatively about how God is at work within us. Stories, songs, music and poetry all help us to meditate.

You can lose yourself in a story and then deep in the drama suddenly see yourself in a new light through some reaction or emotion.

You can find yourself haunted by the line of a song that catches a mood of melancholy or elation which takes you to a new level of self-awareness.

You can be caught up in music so sublime that it takes you out of yourself and transports you to a transcendent place.

You can enter into a poem and dive into its meaning deeper than the poet ever imagined.

Whenever this happens we should cultivate the leisure 'to stand and stare', to meditate, so that 'my heart shall muse of understanding'.

This day on my walk I stood gazing at a field of wild wheat daubed with silk-red poppies and dotted by yellow-hearted white daises. I narrowed my eyes for the effect of an impressionist painting. Two wires seemed to touch as my emotions engaged with my will. My heart spoke: 'Incline my heart to do thy will.'

Meditate

Think of a song, story, poem, music, painting or photograph that has got beneath your skin. Take time to dwell on it. What does it tell you about yourself? Good or bad, let God see it too.

Psalm 51.10, 17

Make me a clean heart, O God:
and renew a right spirit within me.

The sacrifice of God is a troubled spirit:
a broken and contrite heart, O God, shalt thou not despise.

Repetition is a feature of the life of prayer as we can see in the psalms. Yet again the plea for forgiveness comes with 'Make me a clean heart'. There is a particular religious psyche that is obsessed with sin. There's also a psychological condition where the patient obsesses with self-loathing, and this needs expert medical treatment. Prayers such as these can feed this neurosis.

However, this psalm was composed after a specific incident when David was exposed for his adultery and for complicity in the murder of his lover's husband. The psalm has been immortalized by Allegri who set it to music in his *Miserere*.

The psalm traces the disturbance of the heart by sin. It shows that however much we offend others, the greater offence is against God. It makes the point that even though we are born with a disposition to sin we are still culpable for our specific actions. God reaches down to us with justice and mercy – he sets his face against all that is bad but bathes in compassion all who acknowledge their faults. God is moved by the sight of a 'broken and contrite heart' when the only sacrifice we can hope to offer is our 'troubled spirit'.

Sometimes in our shame we hold back from truthfully acknowledging our guilt. The joy is crushed out of our life, like juice from the trodden grape. But, as God showed David, there is still hope for the heart broken by sin: 'Thou shalt make me hear of joy and gladness: that the bones which thou hast broken may rejoice' (v. 8).

Meditate

Consider a sin you have committed with 'Against thee only have I sinned' (v. 4).

Psalm 53.1, 3

The foolish body hath said in his heart:
There is no God.

God looked down from heaven upon the children of men:
to see if there were any, that would understand, and seek after God.

The Bible offers no arguments for the existence of God. It doesn't engage with the intellectual case for or against. It simply assumes God. It makes me think that the person this psalm has in mind is not the atheist or agnostic who wrestles with questions of faith but the amoral or immoral who lives life defiantly as if there were no God. The 'corrupt' are those who exploit others with no sense of their own accountability or culpability. They feel they can get away with murder. The uncompromising message in the Bible is that even if they do in this life they will not forever.

But here there is also a poignant picture that hints of God's own vulnerability. He looks down from heaven aching to find those who might return his love and seek after him. It reminds me of that scene in Athens when Paul is confronted by the intellectuals of the day at the Areopagus. They loved a good argument and were sceptical of Paul's claim that Jesus had risen from the dead. Paul responds by speaking of the Creator who has given us life 'so that [we] would search for God and perhaps grope for him and find him – though indeed he is not far from each one of us. For "In him we live and move and have our being"' (Acts 17.27–28 NRSV).

God seeks that we should seek him. To help us in that search he has set before us Jesus. It was he who promised, 'Search, and you will find' (Matthew 7.7 NRSV). God will not turn away any seeking heart, no matter how searching its questions.

Pray

Lord, I believe; help thou mine unbelief.   (Mark 9.24 KJV)

Psalm 54.6

An offering of a free heart will I give thee,
and praise thy Name, O Lord:
because it is so comfortable.

In the world of the psalms the worship of God involved the offering of gifts. These were signs of the worshippers' dedication to God. There were rules about the quality and purity of the offerings and the sacrifices.

As we draw near to God in our searching after him we begin to realize how much he has already helped us in that journey.

The psalms were often sung as people made their pilgrimage to the Temple in Jerusalem. At the end of the journey the climax for the pilgrims would be to offer their sacrifice to God.

In a way there are similar milestones in our own journey of faith. There can be 'nights of doubt and sorrow', the landscape can feel at times 'a barren land' and those who 'have not God before their eyes' (v. 3) can be antagonistic. Yet the pilgrim perseveres.

There comes then a moment of arrival and the offering of the sacrifice. It is not the end of the journey for there is the travelling home and further pilgrimages in the future. But the destination of this pilgrimage sees pilgrims dedicating themselves afresh to their divine destiny.

The greatest gift that we can give freely of ourselves is our heart, our will. 'Take my life and let it be consecrated, Lord, to thee' (F. M. Havergal's hymn). The 'offering of a free heart' spontaneously is our response to the offering of God's heart to us through his beloved Son. In him and on the cross we see how much God loves us with all his heart. Jesus is his 'offering of a free heart' to us.

Meditate

Were the whole realm of nature mine
That were an offering far too small.
Love so amazing, so divine,
Demands my heart, my life, my all.

> (Isaac Watts (1674–1748), from 'When I survey the wondrous cross', slightly adapted)

Psalm 55.4, 5, 6

My heart is disquieted within me:
and the fear of death is fallen upon me.
Fearfulness and trembling are come upon me:
and an horrible dread hath overwhelmed me.
And I said, O that I had wings like a dove:
for then would I flee away, and be at rest.

Before you undergo surgery the conversation with the doctor is a sobering experience. Your doctor explains the operation and the risks and asks you to sign the form agreeing to the treatment. I was told clearly and kindly about the risk of a stroke and death.

Faced with your own mortality it is normal for the heart to feel anxious.

You can understand how in the face of such overwhelming dread someone could pray: 'O that I had wings like a dove: for then would I flee away, and be at rest.'

I remember when my diagnosis had sunk in that I too wished that I could escape the whole prospect. For a foolish moment I even thought of declining the whole thing.

For one contemplating the fear of death, this psalm shows the way to respond:

As for me, I will call upon God: and the Lord shall save me.
In the evening, and morning, and at noon-day will I pray,
and that instantly.   (Psalm 55.17–18a)

The discipline of regular daily prayer has dipped in western Christendom. It's good to break out of the prison of legalistic ritual; but it's sad to deprive the heart of the oxygen of spiritual life. The daily cycle exercises the heart in the presence of God.

Would that lovely things like beauty, sex, food and wine led us godward with as much speed and regularity, but they seldom do.

Being deprived of those metaphorical wings and being forced to confront our fears, especially of dying and death, allows the disquieted heart to fly and to fix itself on the promises of God, and, like the sparrow and the swallow of Psalm 84, find a nest and rest at his altar.

Meditation

Meditate on a bird taking flight from danger. Consider what fears make you want to fly away.

Psalm 57.8

My heart is fixed, O God, my heart is fixed:
I will sing, and give praise.

The heart is capable of many functions. The sign of being fixed on God is a song of praise and thanksgiving.

Whatever we fix on to in the end absorbs us, so much so that we become dependent on it. That dependency becomes a way of life, integrated into our being. It's as if we were made to be dependent. 'No man is an island', and even those loners who seem so independent of others often have hidden needs that are met by various fixations.

God intends our dependency to be on him: 'Thou wilt keep him in perfect peace, whose mind is stayed on thee,' said Isaiah (26.3 KJV).

Learning to be dependent on God, to be fixed on him, is the work of a lifetime. We have moments when we happily confess to being affixed but we also know that there are powerful temptations weaning us off him.

Although praise and thanksgiving appear in this psalm as the result of fixing oneself to God, my experience is that they can also become a means of fixing the heart to God. Instead of waiting for erratic emotions to ignite the thanksgiving we can exercise our will to initiate a litany of praise. In sleepless early hours I take the alphabet and praise God for different aspects of his character. Almighty, Beautiful, Compassionate, Delighting in his world. Or sometimes I go from A to Z thanking him swiftly and briefly for different gifts of his providence: X-rays that guided the doctors, Young people of the diocese who prayed for me, the Zoo where we spent hours with our children when we had no garden.

Praise and thanksgiving can become the adhesive that fixes the heart to God.

It can also send you to sleep!

Pray

Taking the alphabet, create your own litany of praise.

Psalm 58.1, 2, 10

Are your minds set upon righteousness, O ye congregation:
and do ye judge the thing that is right, O ye sons of men?
Yea, ye imagine mischief in your heart upon the earth:
and your hands deal with wickedness.

So that a man shall say, Verily there is a reward for the righteous:
doubtless there is a God that judgeth the earth.

It is curious in the modern world that whereas there is great emphasis upon human justice, there is so little acceptance of divine judgement. Yet the two are the opposite sides of the one coin. People seem to resist and even dismiss the idea of God judging us, while at the same time making all sorts of judgements about what is just and unjust in the world. They deny God the very virtue which they themselves vaunt. This moral capacity, conscience, comes from God who as the source of all love necessarily sets his face against all that desecrates his Creation. He is not indifferent, nor surely should he be, to any who violate any one of his creatures and rape the earth. The God of love must act against the cruel and the corrupt, if he is worthy of the name of love.

Interestingly, this is partially acknowledged in the popular question, 'Why doesn't God do something about all the suffering in the world?' It's a plea for God to identify the causes and separate out the bad from the good. The expectation that God should remove from the face of the earth all the causes of evil is predicated on the conviction (rightly) that 'doubtless there is a God that judgeth the earth'.

It was this belief that fired the prophets of the Old Testament who railed against the injustices of their day. 'Ye imagine mischief in your heart upon the earth.' This offends God. It should offend us and at least challenge us to 'set our minds on justice'.

It is impossible to be at one with the God of justice and mercy and not be caught up in the divine dynamic of acting justly, loving mercy and walking humbly before God (Micah 6.8).

Meditate

Recollect when you last felt or said, 'That's not fair.' Consider the principle of justice at stake and what this tells us about the moral universe.

Psalm 61.1, 2

Hear my crying, O God:
give ear unto my prayer.
From the ends of the earth will I call upon thee:
when my heart is in heaviness.

'Hear what comfortable words our Saviour Christ saith unto all that truly turn to him. "Come unto me all that travail and are heavy laden, and I will refresh you."' This is the Gospel invitation at the heart of the service of Holy Communion in the Book of Common Prayer.

Heaviness of heart is a regular human condition. Even the most optimistic and positive of people endure things that weigh down the heart and put pressure on the body. When the heaviness becomes unbearable thoughts often turn to God. What holds us back can be a sense that our life is not in order and we are in no fit state to ask God to come close. Either consciously or otherwise we decide to sort ourselves out first – then we might invite God to enter the house once it has been swept clean. If that is ever our attitude then we shall wait for ever while digging ourselves deeper into the mire.

What is so appealing about this invitation from Jesus is that he accepts us as we are, with the heaviness of all our burdens. It is because we cannot lift the weight in our own strength that he bids us turn to him. The simplicity of the call can offend our pride and self-justification but it cuts through the flesh to the heart. And when it does don't be surprised if it reduces you to tears. That feeling that he accepts you as you are, that you no longer need to prove yourself, in

short, that God loves you, begins to lift the heaviness and refresh
the heart.

Pray

Just as I am
without one plea
but that thou bidst me
come to thee.
O Lamb of God, I come.
   (Charlotte Elliott (1789–1871), slightly adapted)

Psalm 62.4, 8

Their device is only how to put him out whom God will exalt:
their delight is in lies; they give good words with their mouth,
but curse with their heart.

O put your trust in him alway, ye people:
pour out your hearts before him, for God is our hope.

There are two hearts that are polar opposites. The cursing heart
is not always plain to see. It can be well disguised, as in Psalm
55, when the person 'having war in his heart' can speak words
'softer than butter' and 'smoother than oil, and yet be they very
swords' (v. 22). Sometimes you come across people who say all
the right things and yet they leave you feeling uncomfortable.
The devices and desires of their hearts are scheming against
you. The tragedy is that such mischief can be found not just
in the world at large but in the Church. Jesus had no qualms
about exposing such religious hypocrisy.

The other heart can be sorely tempted to retaliate. It can also
be seduced by 'wrong', 'robbery' and 'riches'. But the plea from
God is that even though our own position improves we should
'pour out [our] hearts before him, for God is our hope'.

I love verse 7 as a motto: 'In God is my health, and my glory:
the rock of my might, and in God is my trust.'

As I worried about my own health and what would happen
to me these words drew me in and held me in God.

The healthy heart sees the whole person held in God. By contrast with the cursing heart that vaunts itself by putting others
down, the healthy heart waits upon God, knowing that from

him alone comes salvation. It takes no delight in the demise of the deceitful, although some consolation in the assurance that one day they will be exposed 'as a tottering wall' and 'a broken hedge' (v. 3).

Pray

Lord,
I pour out my heart before thee
for in thee alone
is my health and my glory. Amen.
(based on Psalm 62.8 and 7)

Psalm 64.6, 7, 10

They imagine wickedness, and practise it:
that they keep secret among themselves,
every man in the deep of his heart.
But God shall suddenly shoot at them with a swift arrow:
that they shall be wounded.

The righteous shall rejoice in the Lord, and put his trust in him:
and all they that are true of heart shall be glad.

The fate of the enemy in the psalms is an inescapable motif and a problem for many. The origin of evil and sin has perplexed the human mind since the days of Adam and Eve. The sad truth is that, whatever the cause, the human heart can secretly harbour in its depths imaginable wickedness. How God can allow this state of affairs and how he engages with it have occupied theologians and philosophers for millennia.

The psalms, especially when it comes to the problem of evil, offer nothing like a philosophical explanation. They are more akin to poetry. They use language and images like poets and songwriters. Exploring the origin of evil through the psalms would be as challenging as analysing philosophically the ethics of love from the songs of the Beatles. Not impossible, grateful for the pictures but in need of a greater conceptual framework!

Nevertheless there is a poetic image here about the relationship between those who imagine wickedness and God that bears reflection.

'God shall suddenly shoot at them with a swift arrow: that they shall be wounded.' This speaks to my imagination, saying that God does not give up on those antagonistic to him. The arrow wounds; still it does not kill. It's as if God fires warning shots.

I'm struck by the number of biographies, such as those of Somerset Maugham, novelist and playwright, Kenneth Clark, art historian and William Rees Mogg, journalist, where the person is visited unexpectedly by a vivid spiritual experience which causes him to stop in his tracks. It reads often like a wound to the heart. Maugham and Clark chose not to heed their wound; Mogg concluded that his was an epiphany.

Pray

Behold, I was shapen in wickedness: and in sin hath my mother conceived me. But lo, thou requirest truth in the inward parts: and shalt make me to understand wisdom secretly.

(Psalm 51.5–6)

Psalm 66.16, 17

If I incline unto wickedness with mine heart:
the Lord will not hear me.
But God hath heard me:
and considered the voice of my prayer.

Can we ever find God to be deaf to our prayers? After all, surely he sees and hears all. But this poetic image takes us to the heart of prayer. The life of faith is not about finding the right words or rituals to manipulate fate. That's what the occult tries to do. The life of faith is about communing with God and in that communion discerning his heart's desire. When his becomes our heart's desire we give voice in prayer for things which lie in accordance with his will. If our heart harbours doubtful desires or devious devices it is as impossible for God to grant us these as it would be for the devil to wish us well in our walk with God.

The life of prayer is searching for the heart of God. That's why adoration, confession and thanksgiving should precede supplication. These are the ways to God's heart. Rushing straight to God and bypassing these means of grace makes supplication a hit-and-miss affair. The more we wait on God the more we see his nature and his will.

Another way to pray is to stop yourself asking God for anything until you have imagined what Jesus might ask for if he were in your shoes. He said, 'If you abide in me, and my words abide in you, ask for whatever you wish, and it will be done for you' (John 15.7 NRSV). Abiding is the secret, through adoration, confession and thanksgiving.

Pray

In your heart slowly sing the carol chorus:

O come, let us adore him,
O come, let us adore him,
O come, let us adore him,
Christ the Lord!

> (from the Latin hymn 'Adeste fideles'
> by J. F. Wade (*c.* 1711–86), English translation
> by F. Oakeley (1802–80))

Then when your soul is still before God, say repeatedly:

O Lamb of God, that takest away the sins of the
world,
have mercy upon me and grant me thy peace.

> (adapted from words of the 'Gloria in Excelsis'
> and the 'Agnus Dei', Book of Common Prayer)

Then give thanks thoughtfully to God:

We bless thee for our creation, preservation, and all the
blessings of this life.

> (Book of Common Prayer,
> from 'A General Thanksgiving')

Now listen for the still small voice to tell you what to bring
before God.

Psalm 69.21, 22

Thy rebuke hath broken my heart; I am full of heaviness:
I looked for some to have pity on me, but there was no man,
neither found I any to comfort me.
They gave me gall to eat:
and when I was thirsty they gave me vinegar to drink.

Desolation is when you find yourself estranged from both friends and God. To sense that you are rebuked by God breaks the heart. If ever there were grounds for self-pity then these are they, when no one else will offer you pity or comfort.

When we become aware of such spiritual alienation there is no way out except to come to God: 'As for me, when I am poor and in heaviness: thy help, O God, shall lift me up' (v. 30).

When on the cross Jesus, the Lamb of God, took to himself the sins of the world, he experienced this alienation, as sin came between him and his Father. He felt doubly forsaken, by his friends who deserted him and by his Father who remained silent. He cried out, 'My God, my God, why have you forsaken me?' (Matthew 27.46b; Psalm 22.1 NRSV).

Jesus felt that desolation on our behalf. In the moment of dereliction he was forsaken so that we might never be estranged from God.

Whenever self-pity turns us inward, let the heaviness of our heart bring us to our knees at the foot of the cross. It is only there that our broken heart will be healed.

Pray

Jesu, lover of my soul,
let me to thy bosom fly.
　　　　(Charles Wesley,
　　　　　1707–88)

Psalm 73.1, 20, 25

Truly God is loving unto Israel:
even unto such as are of a clean heart.

Thus my heart was grieved:
and it went even through my reins.

My flesh and my heart faileth:
but God is the strength of my heart, and my portion for ever.

The fact that this psalm continues to agonize over the success of the ungodly reflects how we ourselves struggle continuously to square the problem of evil with our faith in a loving God. 'Then thought I to understand this: but it was too hard for me' (v. 15). Although the psalms offer little insight into the origin of evil they speak unmistakably about its destiny. 'The ungodly' may have their day, 'lusty and strong' (v. 4) and 'come in no misfortune like other folk' (v. 5) but their days are numbered, especially those named in the following psalm who say in their hearts 'Let us make havock' (Psalm 74.5) of God's purposes. God and good are eternal; evil and sin are temporary. That's what the eye of faith sees. 'I went into the sanctuary of God: then understood I the end of these men; Namely, how thou dost set them in slippery places: and castest them down, and destroyest them' (vv. 16–17).

The thought of this brings no joy, however, to the person with 'a clean heart'. On the contrary, it causes their hearts to be 'grieved' – I suppose because, in our heart of hearts, we sense that there but for the grace of God do we all go.

This imponderableness of evil takes the psalmist to ponder this simple truth: 'Whom have I in heaven but thee: and there is none upon earth that I desire in comparison of thee' (v. 24). Not even the prosperity of the ungodly.

Meditate

Hold before yourself and God some image of evil from the media.

Let your response to this cruelty be: 'My flesh and my heart faileth.'

Know now that the source of evil is both temporary and terminal:

'For lo, they that forsake thee shall perish.'

(quoting Psalm 73.25a and 26a)

Psalm 77.3, 6

When I am in heaviness, I will think upon God:
when my heart is vexed, I will complain.

I call to remembrance my song:
and in the night I commune with mine own heart,
and search out my spirits.

The walk with God is seldom straight or level. There are dales and vales. The route through them is not always according to God's mapping. We travel badly sometimes because of our poor sense of moral direction. These journeyings, occasionally with tears, are nevertheless known to God, as Psalm 56 puts it: 'Thou tellest my flittings; put my tears into thy bottle: are not these things noted in thy book?' (v. 8).

Yet there are times when it feels as if the Lord will 'absent himself for ever' (v. 7), as if previous promises have 'come utterly to an end' (v. 8) and as if God has forgotten us or, at least, 'forgotten to be gracious' (v. 9). Such is the heaviness that 'my heart is vexed'. However much we try to reassure ourselves, especially in the dark hours of the night: 'my soul refused comfort' (v. 2). We have all been in that place.

The antidote offered by this psalm which, in my experience, helps as many times as it doesn't, is for the heart to tell the mind to get a grip. Remember the display of God's providence in your life. Remember the worship, the word, the works, the way, the wonders of God. Spell these out and savour them. And if your imagination falters, consider further the waters, the clouds, the thunder, the lightning, the earth and the sea.

The person who wrote this psalm has evidently travelled our road ahead of us. It's here in the Bible as part of God's provision. God knows we need it for the journey when it is neither straight nor level.

In Hebrew, the language of the psalms, there is no word for 'history'. Instead we simply find the word 'remember'.

Meditate

Note in a book, even at the back of this one, the times you remember when God has provided for you. Next time you cannot sleep reach for it and remember.

Psalm 78.9, 37, 73

And not to be as their forefathers, a faithless and
stubborn generation:
a generation that set not their heart aright,
and whose spirit cleaveth not stedfastly unto God.

For their heart was not whole with him:
neither continued they stedfast in his covenant.

So he fed them with a faithful and true heart:
and ruled them prudently with all his power.

This psalm is a saga of the heart. Read it all to get the full and turbulent story of one heart in pursuit of the other, the divine and the human. It spans generations. It shows that the faithlessness of one generation does not mean that God will abandon the next.

The spiritual wanderings of our own culture bear a striking resemblance to the abandonment of values, spiritual and moral, that characterize the stubborn generations in this psalm. Ours is a generation that does not cleave steadfastly to God in spite of the plethora of songs, poems, plays and films that deal with spiritual themes. They reveal a spiritual restlessness, a society in search of a soul, not a heart fixed on God. Our culture's talk about God is often condescending. There is little sense of humility in the polemic of the pundits, a consciousness that they may be addressing their own author. 'They did but flatter him with their mouth: and dissembled with him in their tongue' (v. 36).

The response from God seems to come in a later psalm: 'So I gave them up unto their own hearts' lusts: and let them follow their own imaginations' (Psalm 81.13).

Having surgery and convalescing detaches you from the world and gives you a different perspective. Usually I love current affairs and debate but my enthusiasm waned. I wondered if I was depressed. It often happens after surgery. A small part of me still wanted to engage in the public debate about the issues of moment but the larger part felt stranded on another shore.

But from that place there was a chance to view and to listen at a distance and more objectively. Two things strike me in the evergreen debate about morality. First, there is little clarity about what a common code of morality might now be. Second, there is scarcely any sense of awe in the way people talk about the moral law. It sounds as though everybody just has their own ideas and does 'what was right in their own eyes' (Judges 21.25).

As our society moves forward from the crises involving parliamentarians, journalists, bankers and priests in search of new moral leadership, this is the time to think again about the moral law, its source and its content.

Pray

Lord,
call to power
those of a true and faithful heart
who will rule prudently. Amen.
   (compare Psalm 78.73 (of David the king))

Psalm 84.1, 2

O how amiable are thy dwellings:
thou Lord of hosts!
My soul hath a desire and longing to enter into
the courts of the Lord:
my heart and my flesh rejoice in the living God.

We have an ancient apple tree in the garden. It stands as
sentinel at the entrance to the village. Swallows swoop around
its canopy and sparrows dart through its branches. A primary
school in the diocese dedicated to St Luke gave me a bird-box
which I have nailed near the tree. I imagine St Luke would
approve for he captured vividly the image of Jesus comparing
himself with a nesting bird gathering chicks under her wings.
I wait and wait for any bird to tarry at the box, which they fly
past at great speed. I long for one of them to rest there. But,
so far, in vain.

My disappointment is but a faint reflection of God's unre-
quited longing for us to enter his courts of praise. As Jesus told
us, there is joy in the presence of the angels of God when even
one sinner repents and returns.

Those who make the flight to the house of God, even to serve
as a humble doorkeeper, are promised blessings, for 'the Lord
will give grace and worship, and no good thing shall he withhold from them that live a godly life' (v. 12). That worship has
both our heart and flesh rejoicing in the living God. Soul and
body in unison praising God. Singing hymns can be a mixed
experience, especially when it's the wrong tune! But when the
whole body gives voice to the whole heart in adoration of God

we find ourselves on our way to that place where even one day 'is better than a thousand' (v. 10).

On the Sunday before my operation I was listening to *Sunday Worship* on Radio 4 when my room was invaded by the cleaning team. The radio congregation was singing, 'O Lord my God, when I in awesome wonder'. This was one of the cleaning ladies' favourites! Before long the whole ward was echoing to the cleaners singing 'How great thou art'. This unexpected sound made 'my heart and my flesh rejoice in the living God', which I have to admit was not my first reaction when they came bustling in!

Praise

O Lord my God, when I in awesome wonder
consider all the works thy hand hath made,
I see the stars, I hear the mighty thunder,
thy power throughout the universe displayed.
Then sings my soul,
my Saviour God, to thee,
how great thou art!*

---

* Words based on a Swedish hymn by Carl Boberg (1849–1940), English translation by Stuart K. Hine (1899–1989) from 'How great thou art', copyright © 1953 The Stuart Hine Trust/Kingsway Communications Ltd <tym@kingsway.co.uk>, used by permission.

Psalm 86.11, 12

Teach me thy way, O Lord, and I will walk in thy truth:
O knit my heart unto thee, that I may fear thy Name.
I will thank thee, O Lord my God, with all my heart:
and will praise thy Name for evermore.

The prayer to 'knit my heart unto thee' is as poetic as it is profound. Weaving the sinews of our will into the will of God echoes the prayer of Jesus as he faced the cross: 'Not what I want but what you want' (Matthew 26.39b NRSV). His example shows us that it is far from a light thing to ask God to teach us his way and to promise to walk in his truth. When we reach desperate moments in life we can be heard trying to bargain with God: 'If I get better I will do whatever you want me to do.'

I confess to similar conversations. Then, as I felt I was getting stronger so I began to pray that I would serve God with whatever life I had left in me, do whatever he wanted me to do.

We do not appreciate the true potential of our prayer. Furthermore, as this psalm shows, the knitting of our heart to God takes us to fearing his name. This is not fear as in fright, but as in awe. The heart knit to God reveres his holiness and submits to his perfect will.

We talk of God very casually and write about him as if he were a prescription for our ills. Even in church there's less sense of the majesty, the power and the glory of God. The awe has gone out of our worship and the proper fear has all but disappeared from our heart. How do we recover this right relationship with God? A simple prayer to be repeated often,

'Knit my heart unto thee, that I may fear thy name. Knit my heart . . .'

On my walk home today, as I was praying again about living my life for God, a new thought corrected my prayer. I thought I heard God say, 'Instead of you living your life for me, why not let me now live my life through you?' I told him humbly I would like that, even though I do not know where it will lead.

Meditate

Jesus said, '[The Spirit of truth] will be in you . . . Those who love me will keep my word, and my Father will love them, and we will come to them and make our home with them' (John 14.17 and 23 nrsv).

Open the door . . .

Psalm 90.10, 12

The days of our age are threescore years and ten;
and though men be so strong that they come to fourscore years:
yet is their strength then but labour and sorrow;
so soon passeth it away, and we are gone.

So teach us to number our days:
that we may apply our hearts unto wisdom.

This prayer also swims against the tide of our culture where youthfulness is coveted and ageing dreaded. Yet in spite of the worship of agelessness, where the vitamin pills are the sacraments of the day and the workout a religious ritual, we can never escape the intimations of our own mortality. This psalm encourages us to be realistic about the transience of life.

For some this might be a morbid thought, but here it is a spur to 'apply our hearts unto wisdom'.

Most cultures imagine that wisdom comes with age. Those that lack respect for their senior members deprive themselves of the founts of ancient wisdom. Wisdom is not knowledge. It's not so much about asking why, but how. How should we then live?

In this psalm wisdom comes with numbering our days and seeing ourselves from God's watch. Writing this in the week of my birthday I see that I have 367,020 minutes or 61,320 hours or 2,555 days, or 84 months or 7 years until my 'threescore years and ten'. Approximately four million heartbeats. How have I spent those bygone years? How will I sow these seven? With wheat or weeds? Will they be lean or fat? Or, as St Paul wrote, will I build with wood, hay and stubble or with silver, gold and precious stones (see 1 Corinthians 3.12)? The foundation has been laid, Jesus Christ. Will the building be worthy of his name?

Meditate

Think of the quality of the home built for you in eternity if it were made out of the qualities of your life on earth.

Psalm 94.15, 19

Until righteousness turn again unto judgement:
all such as are true in heart shall follow it.

In the multitude of the sorrows that I had in my heart:
thy comforts have refreshed my soul.

The heart is scarred by sorrow when we see the casualties of injustice. Righteousness is both personal and social. It speaks of and to an individual's dealings with others; it also refers to structures and systems that emerge from and affect the whole of society. The history of the human family reveals a curious divide in the human heart. There have been those whose personal relationships have fallen short of the mark who have championed the cause of justice; and there have been others with impeccable personal lives who have shown little interest in righting the wrongs of injustice in the world.

Both are found wanting in the eyes of God, for 'righteousness and justice are the foundation of [his] throne' (Psalm 89.14 NRSV).

The 'true in heart' are those who follow the path of both personal goodness and social justice. Just as two eyes unite in one sight so both these virtues give us a vision of God's righteous will for the human family.

This divide between the personal and the social has sometimes afflicted the Church where divisions have arisen between those emphasizing personal faith and righteousness and those stressing social action and justice. The truth is that they are two eyes uniting in a single vision.

Taking to heart the sorrows of the world is what God does supremely in Jesus. Where he leads we follow. Often through a vale of tears. But our testimony will be 'thy comforts have refreshed my soul'.

Meditate

> Thus says the LORD:
> Maintain justice, and do what is right,
> for soon my salvation will come.
> (Isaiah 56.1 NRSV)

How will this word from God shape your day?

Psalm 95.1, 8, 10

O come, let us sing unto the Lord:
let us heartily rejoice in the strength of our salvation.

To-day if ye will hear his voice, harden not your hearts:
as in the provocation, and as in the day of temptation
in the wilderness;

Forty years long was I grieved with this generation, and said:
It is a people that do err in their hearts,
for they have not known my ways.

This psalm begins with a fanfare and ends in the plagal cadence of a sung 'amen'. There could hardly be a greater contrast between beginning and end. At the start the heart is rejoicing; by the finish the heart is indicted for its erring and straying like a stubborn goat wandering into the wilderness.

This song of salvation surprises because unlike previous psalms it does not rehearse God's acts of mercy. Instead, it simply celebrates Creation. Christians sometimes narrowcast the grace of God by concentrating solely on the cross of Christ. Even though this is the pivotal point in the history of salvation, there is more to the grace of God than Calvary. All that proceeds from the giving heart of God is grace, beginning with Creation: 'In his hand are all the corners of the earth' (v. 4). Kneeling before the Lord our Maker makes us realize how constantly dependent we are on his grace and how responsible we then are for his Creation.

The desecration of the earth and the turning of many parts of it into a wilderness is the result of people erring in their hearts and ignoring God's ways. Just as the people of God grieved him in the wilderness, so in our generation we also provoke God through our selfish exploitation of the land and the sea. 'The sea is his, and he made it: and his hands prepared the dry land' (v. 5). To rape the earth is not just a crime against future generations, it is a blasphemy, for it is to undo his handiwork.

Meditation

The book of Revelation is a kaleidoscope of images that flash before us to shock and to shake us out of our complacency. Contemplate this picture:

> The time for judging has come ...
> for destroying those who destroy the earth.
> (see Revelation 11.18 NRSV)

Psalm 97.1, 11

The Lord is King, the earth may be glad thereof:
yea, the multitude of the isles may be glad thereof.

There is sprung up a light for the righteous:
and joyful gladness for such as are true-hearted.

Psalm 96 invites us to 'worship the Lord in the beauty of holiness: let the whole earth stand in awe of him' (v. 9). And here we hear that the well-being of the earth flows from our recognition of the sovereignty of God. When creature and Creator are in harmony the whole Creation croons for joy. The test of our love for God is the turning of our back on all that is evil. 'O ye that love the Lord, see that ye hate the thing which is evil' (v. 10).

In this psalm there is no escaping the moral challenge. The true-hearted are called to display God's righteousness in their personal life, in the community and in the earth.

The Book of Common Prayer version of the Lord's Prayer has us praying that 'Thy will be done, in earth as it is in heaven.' 'In' is deeper and more integrated than 'on'. Rather like sailors who talk about in a ship rather than on her. At the core of the prayer is the petition for the earthing of heaven.

This psalm hints at the forthcoming fusion when the Lord's Prayer will be finally answered and heaven shall come down to earth and the two become one.

'The presence of the Lord of the whole earth' (v. 5) will become for the righteous a light 'and joyful gladness for such as are true-hearted' (v. 11).

That will not be the reaction of everybody. Sadly not all of us are committed to righteousness in our personal life, in our community and in the earth. Expecting the unrepentant to welcome that day would be like seeing a vegetarian salivating at the killing of the fatted calf!

Meditate

On a scale of 1 to 10 assess the extent to which you practise the three strands of justice in your personal life, in society and in the earth.

Draw three lines representing your three assessments.

With them make a triangle.

Lay this before God.

Psalm 101.3, 5

When wilt thou come unto me:
I will walk in my house with a perfect heart.

A froward heart shall depart from me:
I will not know a wicked person.

This is the psalm for those with perfect pitch who rise to the moral challenge. But perfection's 'song shall be of mercy and judgement' (v. 1). This is the good news: the perfect heart is one that knows both.

Some are tempted to drive a wedge between divine judgement and divine love. It shows in the popular question: 'But how can a God of love judge?' or 'I believe in the God of love of the New Testament, not the God of judgement in the Old.' Yet there is love and judgement in both Testaments.

Divine judgement – God taking decisive action against evil – flows from divine love as surely as discipline from a loving parent. The opposite of judgement is mercy, and both arise out of the heart of God's love.

Out of love God moves in judgement against evil and sin; out of the same love God moves with mercy to offer forgiveness. The sinner who tastes this meat does indeed have a perfect heart. As the murderer and blasphemer Saul discovered and then declared after his conversion, 'There is therefore now no condemnation for those who are in Christ Jesus' (Romans 8.1 NRSV).

Jesus is the ultimate expression of God's love in mercy and forgiveness. Whenever we hear him say to us, 'Your sins are forgiven', we are, in his words, 'free', 'whole' and 'in peace'. Such is the experience of the perfect heart.

Such a heart is known by the company it keeps. Having rejected the way of pride and arrogance, the marks of a 'froward heart', those who know the Lord's judgement and mercy find themselves repelled by the proud and attracted to the humble. When it's the other way around we need to test the heart again!

Pray

My song is love unknown,
My Saviour's love to me,
Love to the loveless shown,
That they might lovely be.
O who am I, that for my sake
My Lord should take frail flesh and die?
       (Samuel Crossman, *c.*1624–83)

Psalm 102.4

My heart is smitten down, and withered like grass:
so that I forget to eat my bread.

A pelican in the wilderness, an owl in the desert, a sole sparrow sitting on the rooftop, these are the pictures that tell of a soul out of sorts. There's little doubt here that the plight of the smitten heart is the work of God. 'For thou hast taken me up, and cast me down' (v. 10).

The only clue to the heart's demise is the reference to God's 'indignation and wrath' (v. 10) and the inference that this is in response to disobedience. The physical symptoms of loss of appetite, aching bones, weight loss, crying, preoccupation with death all suggest a deeply troubled inner life. However much the psalmist may have brought it upon himself, this trauma of the heart has God's name written all over it.

How he responds is an object lesson for all of us who bring folly on ourselves by straying from God's way.

People don't like to think of God visiting upon us ill-health. Again, it doesn't square with modern notions of love. It is also problematic because there are many physical and psychological diseases which have no spiritual cause and have sound medical explanations.

Nevertheless, the smitten soul can sometimes sense that a withering within is like an unpleasant medicine from God to stimulate the heart, to turn it again to God. The antidote to this dis-ease is simply to call out:

Hear my prayer, O Lord: and let my crying come unto thee. Hide not thy face from me in the time of my trouble: incline thine ear unto me when I call; O hear me, and that right soon.   (Psalm 102.1–2)

Elsewhere in the Old Testament we read:

My child, do not despise the LORD's discipline
or be weary of his reproof,
for the LORD reproves the one he loves,
as a father the son in whom he delights.
                    (Proverbs 3.11–12 NRSV)

And in the New Testament:

He disciplines us for our good, in order that we may share his holiness. Now, discipline always seems painful rather than pleasant at the time, but later it yields the peaceful fruit of righteousness to those who have been trained by it.   (Hebrews 12.10b–11 NRSV)

Prayer

Discipline means learning, so:

Lord,
help me to learn Christ. Amen.

Psalm 104.15

That he may bring food out of the earth,
and wine that maketh glad the heart of man:
and oil to make him a cheerful countenance,
and bread to strengthen man's heart.

God knows what makes the human heart glad! All manner of things including good food and good wine. Yet these are but tokens of God's providence as this psalm makes abundantly clear. It holds before us in poetry the blessings of heaven that God has rained down upon the earth.

Forgive this word which jars with the language of the Prayer Book, but the soul gives thanks here for what is now called the ecosystem. Poetry and prayer reach those places that eco-speak can never touch, and in this psalm we stand with God in all his grandeur and survey his wondrous Creation. 'O Lord, how manifold are thy works: in wisdom hast thou made them all; the earth is full of thy riches' (v. 24)

The dependency of one work upon another reveals the harmony and fine balance in which it all hangs, and complements the utter dependency of all upon God himself. 'When thou lettest thy breath go forth they shall be made: and thou shalt renew the face of the earth' (v. 30).

This divine pledge to renew the face of the earth was taken up in the Gospels by Jesus, the Son of Man, Son of Adam, the one hewn from the earth.

He told his disciples that the Son of Man will come again 'at the renewal of all things' (Matthew 19.28 NRSV). What God has made good but which has been damaged by sin he will renew, transform and perfect. Since 'the Lord shall rejoice in his works' (Psalm 104.31b), so should we. He's given us dominion so that we like priests in Eden should serve and preserve the earth.

Pray

Holy Jesus,
Son of Man,
come in glory
and renew
the face of the earth. Amen.

Psalm 105.3, 25

Rejoice in his holy Name:
let the heart of them rejoice that seek the Lord.

Whose heart turned so, that they hated his people:
and dealt untruly with his servants.

Heart versus heart. The heart can fill up with love or hatred. The greatest challenge for the heart filling up with love is to encounter another whose empty heart fills up with hatred, especially when the focus of the bitterness is love itself.

As this psalm relates, that has been the lot of the people of God from Abraham to David. The Lord gave them a promised land. Yet whenever they sought to take possession of it there were enemies determined to deny them it.

It's a parable of the spiritual life. When we seek to know and to do God's will, constrained by his love, we look for signals signposting the way. It's not unusual for us also to find boulders in our path. We should not interpret these as signs to turn back. Quite the opposite. Opposition only confirms the course set before us.

It is sad that those who seek the Lord should meet flak along the way from both human and spiritual enemies. If we think that an unblemished life of love and good intentions will always be welcomed, we have only to look at Jesus to see how his goodness provoked antagonism.

His reaction presents his followers with one of our greatest moral challenges: to pray for and love our enemies, even as we stand our ground against them.

As for the enemy, as Saul discovered, it's highly dangerous to place yourself in the firing line of such prayer.

Pray

Consider a person or situation that appears to be obstructing your path of faith.

Pray for the conversion of the heart of your enemy.

Psalm 107.12

―――――――•◆•――――――――

He also brought down their heart through heaviness:
they fell down, and there was none to help them.

The disease of this heart is down to rebelling 'against the words
of the Lord' and lightly regarding 'the counsel of the most
Highest' (v. 11). Although God is infinitely long-suffering and
compassionate this should not be confused with indifference
to disobedience. Neither should it lull us into thinking that
he can be presumed upon like a doting grandparent. Should
we ever be tempted to minish** God, then, before he minishes
us, we should take a leaf out of a sailor's log and contemplate
God's power at sea.

The stormy wind and waves put the fear of God into the
sailors 'who reel to and fro, and stagger like a drunken man'
(v. 27) whose 'soul melteth away' (v. 26). The One who charged
nature with such devastating power is more powerful yet. The
physical energy on show in Creation is matched by the force
of the Creator's holy and moral purity. Those who live by the
sea respect it. We should have no less respect for the One who
made it, and stand in awe of his holiness.

Should we feel that we have fallen down in our obedience
and become indifferent to God, then, like the sailor crying
out for help in a storm at sea, we need only to cry out to the
Lord to deliver us out of our distress. The benefits are found
in the blessings of this psalm: 'Whoso is wise will ponder these

―――――

* 'Minish' (v. 39) is an old English word for diminish.

118

things: and they shall understand the loving-kindness of the Lord' (v. 43).

Pray

May the fire of Christ consume all indifference to God,
the light of Christ illumine our vision of God,
the love of Christ enlarge our longing for God,
and the Spirit of Christ empower our service to God. Amen.

(The Liverpool Blessing)

Psalm 108.1

O God, my heart is ready, my heart is ready:
I will sing and give praise with the best member that I have.

I was three weeks into my recuperation when this verse revived me! As in life, so in convalescence there are good days and bad days, like walking on a cloudy summer's day, one moment through a field of sunshine, the next under a canopy of shade.

One particular day that shade had lengthened into the long shadow of death. I felt I was making no progress, I was back on the maximum dose of painkillers and I dreaded the night for fear of not sleeping. Then morning dawned and the familiar round of pills, shower, breakfast, Morning Prayer – and Psalm 108!

These words went straight to my heart and, to take a phrase from Psalm 126.2, 'Then was [my] mouth filled with laughter: and [my] tongue with joy.'

I felt that 'God hath spoken [to me] in his holiness' (v. 7) as if laughing with me at my faint-hearted faith. I could almost imagine him smiling and chiding, 'Get a grip!' I then thanked and praised him for 'the best member that I have'!

A postscript in this psalm notes the value of daily Morning Prayer. It is a way of life that we should not neglect. We cannot wonder at our faint faith if we deny ourselves the means of fortifying it.

Pray

O God,
my heart is ready
to do thy will
and to sing thy praise. Amen.

Psalm 109.21

O deliver me, for I am helpless and poor:
and my heart is wounded within me.

A spiritual battle rages around us. It breaks through into the
material world. It is impossible not to be caught up in it and,
from time to time, to be wounded. Of course, many today
dismiss this as medieval theology, but read the opening stanzas
of this psalm and it does not take much to imagine contemporary parallels. The atrocities uncovered in countries liber-
ated from oppression are evidence of evil.

Lies, hatred and people taking against others 'without a cause'
(v. 2), some even rewarding 'evil for good: and hatred for my
good will' (v. 4). These are not just manifestations of flawed
human nature but evidence of evil endemic in the spiritual
realm. Endemic but not eternal, for Satan's days are 'few' rela-
tive to eternity.

You can understand the reaction of the wounded to their
assailants: may God 'root out the memorial of them from off
the earth' (v. 14).

There's an old adage about the sinner being like one who
spits into the air. That captures the fate of the evil one in this
psalm who finds it all falling back on his own head.

'His delight was in cursing, and it shall happen unto him
(v. 16), 'and it shall come into his bowels like water, and like
oil into his bones' (v. 17). These strong images speak of a world
of commandment, conscience and consequence and of a moral
universe where eventually we reap what we sow. But there is
always compassion for those who turn. There is also healing

for the wounded from the Wounded Healer himself who constantly found himself caught up in the spiritual battle between good and evil, and lived beyond death to tell the tale.

Pray

Lord,
clad me in armour
to withstand the wiles
of the powers of darkness
through Jesus Christ. Amen.

Psalm 111.1

I will give thanks unto the Lord with my whole heart:
secretly among the faithful, and in the congregation.

The art of gratitude is a grace given by God. George Herbert
(1593–1633) expressed it beautifully.

> Thou that hast giv'n so much to me,
> Give one thing more, a grateful heart.
> See how thy beggar works on thee
> By art.
>
> Not thankful, when it pleaseth me;
> As if thy blessings had spare days:
> But such a heart, whose pulse may be
> Thy praise.   (first and last verses of 'Gratefulness')

But if from the heart we cannot echo the enthusiasm of the
opening verse of this psalm we should look to the grounds of
gratitude laid out in the rest of the psalm. These grounds are
'the works of the Lord' (v. 2). To appreciate any one of these
would lead to thanking God in part; appreciating them all leads
to thanksgiving with the whole heart.

I number at least seven.

First, justice; in a world of so much unfairness, it is a relief
to know that justice will one day triumph and endure for ever
(v. 3).

Second, mercy; in a world of sinners, dependent on God's
forgiveness, his grace always 'ought to be had in remembrance'
(v. 4).

Third, food; in a world where millions starve, we see that through earth's larder God has made ample provision for all to be fed (v. 5a).

Fourth, the covenant; in a world of so many broken relationships, God's promise to love us will never be broken (v. 5b).

Fifth, the commandments; in a world where all have a conscience there are moral laws to guide us (v. 7).

Sixth, truth; in a world where poets, songwriters and philosophers search for it, God responds by giving us a true person, Jesus (v. 8).

Seventh, redemption; in a world where the media mercilessly exploit our failures, God pledges to redeem us (v. 9).

These works of the Lord are great but not exhaustive. Yet they stir us to be in awe of God. Such 'fear of the Lord is the beginning of wisdom' and the beginning of thanksgiving (v. 10).

Pray

Link each one of the seven 'gratitudes' to a day of the week, the first being Sunday. Take whichever one is set for today. Ask God to grant you a grateful heart for this work of his.

Psalm 112.7, 8

He will not be afraid of any evil tidings:
for his heart standeth fast, and believeth in the Lord.
His heart is established, and will not shrink:
until he see his desire upon his enemies.

A sign of the heart established in God is that it does not shrink. Nor is it 'afraid of any evil tidings'. The reason for this is that 'unto the godly there ariseth up light in the darkness' (v. 4). That light is none other than the mercy of God which rescues us from the darkness.

Saul was an example of someone who lived in the darkness, from which he was then rescued by an encounter with Jesus. This is his testimony: 'He has rescued us from the power of darkness and transferred us into the kingdom of his beloved Son, in whom we have redemption, the forgiveness of sins' (Colossians 1.13–14 NRSV).

In the end, there are only two worlds, light and darkness. Entering into God's mercy is like walking from a windowless, darkened room into daylight. It can be blinding and overwhelming. Some conversion experiences are like that – Saul's was – though for others the light dawns slowly from their childhood.

But it is because we ourselves have experienced the warmth of the light that we need not fear the cold of dank darkness. 'We've been there, done that', and know that dawn trumps the night. Many believe in the reality of good and evil, thinking they are equal in force. Christians, however, believe that the days of darkness will one day vanish, banished by the inexorable light of God, proving the inequality between good and evil and the power of light over darkness. Even a small candle lit low dents the darkness of a cave.

Pray

Lighten our darkness, we beseech thee, O Lord; and by thy great mercy defend us from all perils and dangers of this night; for the love of thy only Son, our Saviour, Jesus Christ. Amen.

(Book of Common Prayer,
the Third Collect at Evening Prayer)

Psalm 119.2, 7

Blessed are they that keep his testimonies:
and seek him with their whole heart.

I will thank thee with an unfeigned heart:
when I shall have learned the judgements of thy righteousness.

'Blessed be he that cometh in the Name of the Lord: we have wished you good luck' (Psalm 118. 26). How words change their meaning! 'Good luck' has a ring of superstition about it today. Yet in Psalm 118 'luck' is associated with the household of faith and synonymous with blessing. It comes to those who keep his testimonies and seek the Lord with their whole heart.

If the invitation to seek the Lord still seems too abstract then this psalm offers some practical steps to shape your spiritual life: 'keep his testimonies'. This has a wide range of meaning and includes recollecting all that God has done for us both generally (for everybody) and specifically (for me personally).

Because the mind is forgetful and our spiritual memory often dull it is good to write down those episodes when we have been conscious of God's providence and intervention. Even as you have travelled through these thoughts about the heart it is worth noting down those times that the psalms have spoken to your own heart. This will encourage you to thank him 'with an unfeigned heart', sincerely, and to seek him wholeheartedly.

Meditate

Turn back to one of the psalms that spoke into your world.
   What did it tell you about yourself?
   What did it suggest to you about God?

Pray

Lord,
with these thoughts
teach me thy way. Amen.

Psalm 119.10, 11

With my whole heart have I sought thee:
O let me not go wrong out of thy commandments.
Thy words have I hid within my heart:
that I should not sin against thee.

It is one thing to *think* a thought, it is quite another to bury it and hide it in the heart. Years ago people would learn verses of the Bible off by heart; sadly this is no longer in vogue educationally. Pity! We deprive ourselves. Memorizing a verse, meditating on it, musing over it on a walk, making it part of yourself and thus hiding it in your heart nourishes your faith. What is more, in a time of crisis when it is impossible to summon up the physical and mental energy to pray, these heart-hidden words come to the surface from within.

This is the place that I found myself in when news of my surgery sank in. I fell back on verses that I knew by heart and on these prayers that I had memorized.

Over the years in Liverpool I have hidden these prayers in my heart:

- Father, Father, Holy Father,
  Father, Father, Righteous Father.
- Lord Jesus Christ, Son of God, have mercy on me a sinner.
- Holy Jesus, Son of Man,
  come in glory
  and renew the face of the earth.

- Come, Holy Spirit,
  and fill me with all the fullness of God
  that I might know the immeasurable greatness of
  your power in those who believe.
- Holy Trinity,
  Holy Father, Holy Jesus, Holy Spirit,
  thank you for the grace of all that you have given
  and for the generosity of all that you
  are giving to me, to us and to all Creation.

Memorize

Return to one of the verses of the psalms that has touched your
heart and commit it to your memory and heart.

Psalm 119.32

I will run the way of thy commandments:
when thou has set my heart at liberty.

Freedom. We may not have been born free, but for freedom we were made and redeemed. Walking near our cottage where I was convalescing I penned these couplets:

> Free as a fly that dodges the swat, free as a fish that
>   misses the plot,
> Free as the wind that snaps the twig, free as the
>   stream that skirts the brig,
> Free as the smoke that swirls from the fire, free as
>   the flames that dance with desire,
> Free as the smile that flits from your lip, free as the
>   laughter that unlocks your grip,
> Free as the love that sets others free, free as the soul
>   that yearns to be me.

Jesus came into the world to set us free from anything that enslaves us, everything from sin to death. But this liberty has strings. It comes with intentions. It is a freedom both from and to. Just as a reformed prisoner might say on release from prison, 'I'm free now and determined to go straight', so we are set free from sin to live our life according to God's law.

Just as birds are free to fly anywhere but cannot fly under water so we are free to live within the curtilage of God's laws.

It is through living within these boundaries that God intends us to become the very person that our soul yearns to be. The measure of the liberty that our heart has found is the degree of desire our heart has to 'run the way of thy commandments'.

Jesus said, 'If the Son makes you free, you will be free indeed' (John 8.36 NRSV).

A prayer

Whenever a prisoner writes to me as Bishop to Prisons I send this prayer. Prisons come in different forms, even a hospital bed!

> Lord Jesus, friend to all in prison,
> for you too were punished and imprisoned
> (even though you did no wrong),
> come close to me.
> Banish all my fears,
> breathe peace into my mind
> and hope into my heart.
> Take care of all I hold dear,
> for your love is stronger than
> these prison gates,
> and keep us safe from harm.
> Show me the path that leads to freedom,
> inside and out,
> and bless me today and for ever. Amen.

Psalm 119.34, 36

Give me understanding, and I shall keep thy law:
yea, I shall keep it with my whole heart.

Incline my heart unto thy testimonies:
and not to covetousness.

Like the eye, the heart can wander. Sometimes it seems as if the eye has the heart on a lead! Like pushing a child on a tricycle and constantly needing to reset the direction with the handlebars, so the heart needs steering. We have to set the heart's direction which is why we find in this psalm the prayer, 'Incline my heart unto thy testimonies'. But as well as turning the heart towards God's 'testimonies', we also need to turn it away from distractions.

Covetousness is when the heart wanders after other people's possessions. It may surprise you or even disappoint you that this far on into the psalms we're still talking about monitoring the heart. Why is it not yet knitted and fixed?

Like the bodily organ it continually responds to stimuli and its environment. It is both dynamic and responsive. However knitted and fixed to God our heart has become we are forever meeting new situations and challenges. These stretch the heart and, as with the physical member, it grows stronger through exercise.

One of these exercises is encountering people whose lot in life fares better than our own, or so it seems. It can be galling when not only do they disregard God but they make a show of it. We can also find ourselves coveting the lot of people of faith, their gifts and their achievements. This is the spiritual equivalent of the physical heart taking a long, slow walk uphill! Facing up to covetousness, then asking God to incline our heart to him, is a vital spiritual exercise through which we grow in faith.

Pray

Think first and honestly about one person you covet or have coveted.

O turn away mine eyes, lest they behold vanity: and quicken thou me in thy way. (Psalm 119.37)

Psalm 119.58

I made my humble petition in thy presence with my whole heart:
O be merciful unto me, according to thy word.

The more aware we become of the presence of God, the more humble our praying. The more humble our prayers, the more in accordance with the will of God will they be made.

I fear that so much praying is prattling, like excited or even desperate children bombarding parents with their demands. If only we could learn to wait humbly in the presence of God before opening the mouth of our heart.

Some years back I travelled the Diocese of Liverpool holding evenings in different Deaneries, teaching about prayer. At the end of every night I led us all in a spiritual exercise.

> Draw a circle around you with yourself at the centre. Then place on the circumference all that weighs upon you. Look around and consider carefully those concerns. Let their weight bear down upon you. Then walk away from the centre and out of the picture. Imagine now Jesus entering the circle and standing at the centre in your place. Imagine how he would pray for the things that worry you.

In doing this now I find the weight lifting from my shoulders at the sight of Jesus taking his place at the centre of my life. As I imagine his reaction I sense that his response to people is 'she's mine', 'he's mine'; and to situations, 'in time', 'in my time'. Each of us will hear his voice in our own way.

The point is to find a humble beginning to our praying.

Prayer

We do not presume to come to this thy Table, O merciful Lord, trusting in our own righteousness, but in thy manifold and great mercies.

(Book of Common Prayer, from the Holy Communion)

Psalm 119.69, 70

The proud have imagined a lie against me:
but I will keep thy commandments with my whole heart.
Their heart is as fat as brawn:
but my delight hath been in thy law.

Fat hearts are bad for you, physically and spiritually. This psalm is a spiritual health warning for those whose heart 'is as fat as brawn'. Pride is the symptom of a gross heart. The problem is that the proud do not always see their pride, it escapes their notice like a bald patch on the back of the head. If it creeps up on us how do we protect ourselves from this the most insidious of the seven deadly sins? 'O learn me true understanding and knowledge: for I have believed thy commandments' (v. 66).

'Learn me' not just teach me. It's a plea for God to integrate into the whole fabric of our life his truth. Instead of spreading manure on the surface of the soil, dig it in and turn it over. Practically, it means promising to 'keep thy commandments with my whole heart'. Unfortunately they are hardly ever heard in church today and most members might be hard put to recall all ten.

So here they are. They are the antidote to pride and a fat heart. Take time to think them into your life. Dig them in. Convalescence is like a harvested field about to be ploughed for a new crop. Now is the time for it to be turned over.

I am the LORD your God, who brought you ... out of the house of slavery; you shall have no other gods before me. You shall not make for yourself an idol ... You shall not bow down to them or worship them; for I the LORD your God am a jealous God ... You shall not make wrongful use of the name of the LORD your God, for the LORD will not acquit anyone who misuses his name. Remember the sabbath day, and keep it holy. For six days you shall labour and do all your work ... For in six days the LORD made heaven and earth, the sea, and all that is in them, but rested the seventh day ... Honour your father and your mother, so that your days may be long in the land that the LORD your God is giving you. You shall not murder. You shall not commit adultery. You shall not steal. You shall not bear false witness against your neighbour. You shall not covet your neighbour's house ... or anything that belongs to your neighbour.   (Exodus 20.2–17 NRSV)

Prayer

Lord, have mercy upon us, and write all these thy laws in our hearts, we beseech thee.

(Book of Common Prayer,
response to the Ten Commandments)

Psalm 119.80

O let my heart be sound in thy statutes:
that I be not ashamed.

Shame has all but disappeared from our society like vinyl records and black Bakelite phones. Symptomatic, I think, of a culture that would like to shrug off guilt in the quest to feel good. Today's mantra is that nobody should ever feel bad about themselves. This is the ultimate sin of modernity, to blaspheme against the god Ego. Bow down and praise yourself and don't let anyone trespass against you!

Well, the desire to feel no shame is a godly one. Shame is an uncomfortable and distressing condition. But the antidote to shame is not the indulgence of the wild self but the taming of its transgressions by God's laws, which produces 'a sound heart'.

A sound heart is the vital organ that pumps blood around the body. As a diabetic I know the danger of the blood failing to reach the extremities – with serious consequences. The consequence of an unsound spiritual heart is spiritual diabetes whereby the truth of the faith fails to touch every aspect of our life. A classic example would be going to church on Sunday and closing the door on our faith on Monday.

Just as we need a sound heart to pump the blood, so we need a sound spiritual heart beating at the centre of our faith, pumping its truth into the furthermost reaches of our life. It should oxygenate not just our beliefs but our relationships, our ambitions, our money, our everything. Such is the path to self's fulfilment.

Pray

Thy hands have made me and fashioned me: O give me understanding, that I may learn thy commandments.

(Psalm 119.73)

Psalm 119.111, 112

Thy testimonies have I claimed as mine heritage for ever:
and why? they are the very joy of my heart.
I have applied my heart to fulfil thy statutes alway:
even unto the end.

There's a joyless religion that should be avoided like the plague. There's a certain personality that obsesses with detail; it becomes preoccupied with rules and ritual; it prefers the letter of the law to the spirit of the law. Jesus clashed with this sort of person all the time. Religious regulations became an end in themselves rather than a means to bringing life: think of the Pharisees who objected to Jesus healing people on the day of rest because it looked like work. Jesus dealt with such killjoys by telling them that the Sabbath was made for the sake of humanity, not the other way around.

These killjoys give religion a bad name and make people on the fringe of faith run a mile. But sadly religion can recruit such people and reinforce such attitudes.

How can we be sure our own heart isn't tied up in a legalistic straitjacket? With a simple question: where's the joy?

If our religion is joyless we need to revisit the heart. If our attitude to God's testimonies in Creation, the Commandments and conscience is dutiful but joyless there's something fundamentally awry. It probably means we've found the law but not the love behind it. The loveless lawful heart can be a cruel instrument and crush the humanity out of religion.

Earlier in this psalm we find the prayer, 'O quicken me after thy loving-kindness: and so shall I keep the testimonies of thy mouth' (v. 88). As Jesus said, 'If you love me, you will keep my commandments' (John 14.15 NRSV). Love comes before the law. When our lore looks like love's law then joy visits the heart.

Pray

Lord, restore unto me the joy of thy salvation.

(cf. Psalm 51.12 KJV)

Psalm 119.145, 161

I call with my whole heart:
hear me, O Lord, I will keep thy statutes.

Princes have persecuted me without a cause:
but my heart standeth in awe of thy word.

The word of God comes to us in several ways. Supremely in Jesus who was 'the Word made flesh' (cf. John 1.14). Without the Bible Jesus is a contentless word. It is Scripture that gives substance and meaning to his life, death and resurrection. Jesus' own attitude to the Old Testament was to treat it as God's word, so that the law, the psalms and the prophets spoke to him with divine authority. Which is why this psalm tells us, 'my heart standeth in awe of thy word'.

Having read so many psalms it may seem a little late to enquire into your own attitude to the Bible. Yet having got this far it's a good place to reflect on what has caused you to stay the course. Has there been any sense of awe in the reading of these psalms?

It is the heart and not the mind that stands in awe. The mind will rightly ask all sorts of academic and intellectual questions about the Bible. The heart has a different purpose. It is the seat of the will. The Bible has the power to search the heart and to challenge the will to respond to God. God speaks to us in Scripture through history, story, law, letters, prophecy, poetry, psalms, songs, visions and dreams. He engages our heart. He tests our will. The Bible is the sacrament of the word, a means of grace so that we might respond to the voice of God. In reading these verses from the psalms you may well have begun to sense God's claim on your life. In which case your heart will already have called upon him and begun to stand in awe of him.

Meditate

Lay before God one episode when your will has been challenged by his word.

Retrace your steps and reflect on what has flowed from it.

Psalm 125.4

Do well, O Lord:
unto those that are good and true of heart.

God spoke through the prophet Jeremiah to his people: 'I will rejoice in doing good to them, and I will plant them in this land in faithfulness, with all my heart and all my soul' (Jeremiah 32.41 NRSV).

The Lord is committed to his children with all his heart. This should not surprise us. If God longs for us to love him with all our heart, soul and strength surely he will not love us any less so. And if we doubt it we have the cross to prove the height, depth and breadth of his love. It is on those promises that we find the confidence to pray, 'Do well, O Lord, unto me', but with a number of proper qualifications.

First, what we consider to be in our best interests may not be so seen from God's throne. So, when we pray for God to do well by us and for us, we with our finite wisdom must defer to his infinite wisdom. Just as parents, out of love, cannot give to their children all that their infant hands reach out for, so God's love withholds those things which, unbeknown to us, are not for our good ultimately.

Second, the promise belongs to the 'good and true of heart'. Sometimes we hold back from God even when we pray. This clouds our spiritual judgement and dulls our spiritual imagination so that we ourselves do not see as clearly as we could what is best to pray for.

Third, if our heart is not 'good and true' it could be that we are holding on to some secret desire that we have not yet confessed. This leaves the heart lukewarm and unreceptive to the will of God. Be sure the plans God has for his people are for our good and for his glory.

Meditate

Write these two sayings on your heart by memorizing them:

If you then, who are evil, know how to give good gifts to your children, how much more will your Father in heaven give good things to those who ask him!

(Matthew 7.11 NRSV)

He who did not withhold his own Son, but gave him up for all of us, will he not with him also give us everything else?

(Romans 8.32 NRSV)

Psalm 139.23

Try me, O God, and seek the ground of my heart:
prove me, and examine my thoughts.

This psalm speaks of the intimate knowledge God has of each of us. Jesus said as much, in that even the hairs on our head are numbered. There are no other words that match the truth and beauty of this prayer so allow me to say only why it always leaves my soul in a crumpled heap.

Even though we are made in the image of our Trinitarian God to live and find our identity in community (the Africans call this Ubuntu) there is while we sojourn on earth an aloneness in being human. In friendship, in marriage, in fellowship, in comradeship, in teams and in different forms of community we experience bonds of affection. Yet even in marriage, which brings us closest to that oneness with another human being, the two never completely lose their singleness because that last step into death from the land of the dying to the world of the truly alive is made alone. However deep the love, however bonded the union, we never escape that shadow. Moreover, as we bear our different burdens and share them with those who love us there is an inner atrium inaccessible to the nearest and dearest where we live with all the furnishings of our motives, actions and consequences. The solace offered by lovers serenades the soul at its door but cannot remove the furniture. We alone live with the fullness of our own story, and are known fully by no other – except the Lord of Psalm 139, who 'hast fashioned me behind and before: and laid thine hand upon me' (v. 4).

It is in that knowledge which is 'too wonderful and excellent for me' (v. 5) that my soul bows in reverence. It is there on that ground that my heart rests, 'searched', 'known' and 'fashioned'.

So a prayer

I will give thanks unto thee, for I am fearfully and wonderfully made. (Psalm 139.13)

Psalm 141.4

———•◆•———

O let not mine heart be inclined to any evil thing:
let me not be occupied in ungodly works with the men that
work wickedness,
lest I eat of such things as please them.

The strong language of the psalms is not for the faint-hearted. It can repel those who come to the psalms seeking sincerely to find or to strengthen their faith. References to 'evil', to the 'ungodly' and to 'wickedness', and imprecations asking that the enemy should be exterminated seem to jar with the meekness of faith. This jangling language was in the hearts and mouths of these pilgrims because of what they encountered as they sought to claim the land God had promised them. The tribes that fought them were infamous for their abuse and immorality. As they journeyed from Egypt to 'the land of milk and honey' they were hemmed in by people whose values and beliefs were not only very different but intimidating. The temptation to compromise was strong.

Their journey through the wilderness is a parable of the progress we all make through life. Throughout we meet others who, through intimidation or infatuation, through threat or influence, can throw us off course. My own experience is that these temptations can often come on the heels of greater commitment and deeper spiritual insight.

In a way, just as the oasis of Jesus' baptism was followed by a wilderness of temptation we can expect similar threats to our faith. These need to be named and faced and resisted robustly. But we should not be surprised. If there is a devil, a sinister spiritual force that presses upon us personally, we should turn these psalms against him and confidently protect ourselves with 'the whole armour of God' (Ephesians 6.11–17 NRSV).

The fact that so few Christians take seriously this dimension of the spiritual life is one of the wiles of the devil.

Pray

And lead me not into temptation, but deliver me from evil. For thine is the kingdom, the power, and the glory, for ever and ever.   (adapted from Matthew 6.13 KJV)

Psalm 143.4

Therefore is my spirit vexed within me:
and my heart within me is desolate.

In the New Testament there are many adjectives that describe God but only four nouns. God is Fire, Light, Love and Spirit. It is these four manifestations of God that minister to the desolate heart.

Fire speaks of God's judgement, which will one day destroy all those forces that vex the soul. It will consume antipathy and indifference to God, the enemies of faith.

Light that shines from God will not only dispel darkness in and around us, it will also illumine our vision of God, assisting us to see him more clearly.

Love that is God invites us to walk with him; his loving kindness is constantly wooing us out of our loneliness.

Spirit that is God means that his power is present and available to us as he leads us in our weakness to the kingdom of justice and mercy.

The causes of our desolation – our enemies, the darkness, our loneliness, our weakness – meet their remedy in the riches of God's character. Thus the psalm encourages us to pray: 'Quicken me, O Lord, for thy Name's sake' (v. 11).

Pray

May the fire of Christ consume all indifference to God,
the light of Christ illumine our vision of God,
the love of Christ enlarge our longing for God,
and the Spirit of Christ empower our service to God. Amen.

(The Liverpool Blessing)

Psalm 147.3

He healeth those that are broken in heart:
and giveth medicine to heal their sickness.

God's healing is both spiritual and physical. We can pray for God to heal both the broken heart and the broken body.

The health that comes to our broken bodies through modern medicine is by comparison with the age of the psalms and the time of Jesus nothing short of miraculous. When I allow myself to think of the details of my surgery, even my squeamish mind baulks in wonder! These results of human ingenuity are ultimately gifts from God who made us. When we are struck down by illness we naturally pray for God to make us well. We look to the healings of Jesus and ask him to touch our lives in the same way. The difference between then and now is that the Gospels record Jesus healing all who asked; in our day some are healed and some are not.

It's important to understand that when Jesus healed he was not saying that no one would ever die; rather, his miracles were giving out a new message. In effect he was saying to a culture where people died very young, 'You think disease and death are the last words on human existence, but I have news for you, good news, a day is coming when all these things shall be in the past' – and to prove it he healed them.

As we feel the frailty of our physical bodies even in an age of miraculous medicine and long for healing, the eye of faith trains its sight on another horizon when through death we take on new 'spiritual bodies'. They have continuity with our physical bodies and are indwelt by the same spiritual heart.

Through the resurrection Jesus opens the gate to a new world where heaven and earth are fused and God wipes away the tears from our eyes, promising an end to death and to pain, physical, spiritual, emotional and mental. All the enemies of wholeness will be removed 'and we shall dwell in the house of the Lord for ever' (cf. Psalm 23.6b).

Pray

Lord, feed me in a green pasture:
and lead me forth beside the waters of comfort.
(based on Psalm 23.2)

Psalm 149.4

For the Lord hath pleasure in his people:
and helpeth the meek-hearted.

What a glorious place to end! The thought that God takes pleasure in us supplants all those other false notions of God being rather fed up with us. The problem with low self-esteem, which afflicts so many of us, is that we project this on to how God must see us. When we couple this with all that the psalms say about sin we can come away with the idea that God must hate us, or at least, find us all a trial. Yet God's starting point is not hatred. The beginning of our relationship with him is the pleasure that he takes in creating us and relating to us. Sin is an issue because it dents the pleasure, not because it reinforces any hatred on his part.

Our creation was an act of sheer goodness, his making us a mystery of love. From the beginning, indeed even before the foundation of the world, he has delighted in us and made provision for us. His intention to rid the world of sin and evil is that this delight and pleasure might abound in him and in us for eternity.

As an earlier psalm captured: 'Thou shalt shew me the path of life; in thy presence is the fulness of joy: and at thy right hand there is pleasure for evermore' (Psalm 16.12).

As for the meek, Jesus reiterates the promise of the psalm. Not only will God help them, it is they who will inherit the earth. The heaven where we are bound will have come down to earth where God will dwell with us and we with him as he declares with the grace of the constant Creator, 'See, I am making all things new' (Revelation 21.5 NRSV). How glorious to place ourselves under this banner of love.

Praise

Glory be to God on high, and in earth peace, good will towards men. We praise thee, we bless thee, we worship thee, we glorify thee, we give thanks to thee for thy great glory, O Lord God, heavenly King, God the Father Almighty.

O Lord, the only-begotten Son Jesu Christ; O Lord God, Lamb of God, Son of the Father, that takest away the sins of the world, have mercy upon us. Thou that takest away the sins of the world, have mercy upon us. Thou that takest away the sins of the world, receive our prayer. Thou that sittest at the right hand of God the Father, have mercy upon us.

For thou only art holy; thou only art the Lord; thou only, O Christ with the Holy Ghost, art most high in the glory of God the Father. Amen.

(Book of Common Prayer, Holy Communion)

Postscript to the Psalms

Behold, thou desirest truth in the inward parts:
and in the hidden part thou shalt make me to know wisdom.

This verse (Psalm 51.6 KJV) does not come with the word 'heart' in the psalm version of the Book of Common Prayer but for me it has been at the centre of my faith. Even though the Hebrew is not clear, the words capture the transparency of our relationship with God. 'No secrets are hid' from his eyes. He sees into us and knows us more fully than we know ourselves. Coming to a crisis in life when so much is stripped away brings us nearer to our true self. In our inadequacy to the trial we feel our frailty.

The reason, I believe, that God desires truth in the inward being is that we cannot progress or mature unless we have self-knowledge. We can delude ourselves on a summer's day when all seems right with the world; but in the storm at sea that threatens our life, fears surface from the depths and tell us more about our true self.

Like many believers I have found that it is the confronting of 'truth in the inward being' that sets a new path both in my faith and in my life. When our Lord promised us the help of the Holy Spirit it was for understanding the truth about God and about our self.

A prayer that has sustained me over the years is one by Henry VI:

O Lord Jesus Christ, who hast created and
   redeemed me
and hast brought me unto that which now I am,
thou knowest what thou wouldst do with me:
do with me according to thy will
for thy tender mercy's sake.

It recognizes our place and purpose within the sovereignty and mercy of God, two themes that are writ large throughout the psalms. There is great liberty to be found in abandoning all that you know of yourself into the tender embrace of God.

That communion with God takes place within the 'secret heart'. This is the court where we are known as by no other; it is also the mode in which our heart is formed, that is, secretly. So secret is that formation that we are unlikely to know all the influences that have shaped it.

It was not until my twenties that I discovered that an elderly aunt had prayed for me every day of my life from my baptism as a baby. The amethyst of her necklace forms the heart of my episcopal ring, reminding me daily of her life of prayer.

Even those who can testify to a Damascus road conversion might not know their full story. I wonder how much Paul realized his persecuted relatives Junius and Andronicus had prayed for him prior to his conversion. The mystery of our faith, its origin and nurture, is so great that we cannot fully fathom it. Yet this greatness humbles the heart to pray, 'Do with me according to thy will.'

As a bishop I have played my part in synods and councils, committees and consultations addressing the future of the Church. In this latest episode of feeling 'I should utterly have fainted' and of tarrying 'the Lord's leisure' I begin to wish I had spent more time in and on 'the secret heart'. The future energy of the Church of England depends much more than we realize on the heart of her members. The psalms encourage us to pray for the heart, to ask God to visit, to fix, to knit and to comfort it. The renewed heart is the key to the renewal of the Church, and to the awakening of Christian faith.

I am not calling for an aggressive evangelism but for a quiet transfusion of faith that inspires the believer and the seeker. The English are a tolerant people forged out of the migration of tribes and peoples over thousands of years. Just as its national character has been melded, so too its spirituality and its Christian faith have evolved through Celtic, Catholic and Reformed influences. As someone born of a Welsh father and a Scots mother, who for half a century has lived and worked in England, and whose own evangelical faith has been scarified by catholic and liberal encounters, I believe that the faith of the Church of England advances by osmosis, not oppression.

In city and village, in town and suburbia the parish church still occupies a unique position, admittedly to different degrees in different places. In areas abandoned by others and bereft of pub, bank, post office, school and surgery, the Church is there still acting as convenor of the people and offering community, continuity, civic leadership and communion with God.

It is this communion with God of which the psalms sing with their ancient wisdom. Heart speaks to heart. This was pressed upon me as a child. As a choirboy in the parish church of Sully in South Wales, I remember the vicar inviting me to choose a hymn on our last Sunday before my father's posting to Scotland. I chose:

> O come to my heart, Lord Jesus,
> there is room in my heart for thee.
> > (Emily E. Elliott, 1836–97, from
> > 'Thou didst leave thy throne')

Then as a server in the chapel of my military boarding school in Dover the chaplain gave me a recording of Canterbury Cathedral Choir singing 'Jesu, joyance of my heart'.

> Jesu, joyance of my heart,
> Blessed Jesu;
> Bliss unto my soul thou art,
> Holy Jesu;
> Sure defence from Satan's dart,
> Sweetest Jesu.
>> (G. R. Woodward,
>> 1848–1934)

Throughout my spiritual journey these two hymns have drawn me deeper into communion with God especially in times of challenge or crisis. There is a simplicity about the sentiment of the heart that cuts through everything. 'Jesu, joyance of my heart' was sung at my consecration as bishop in York Minster. Whether you're a seven-year-old chorister or a bishop, these hymns bring your heart to the same place and to the same person, and into holy communion with God.

Although the Church has many important functions in society, her essence is Holy Communion. Through the beauty of our worship and the goodness of our redeemed humanity we ourselves are to be the invitation to others to open their own hearts to God and to find him, to 'see the goodness of the LORD in the land of the living' (Psalm 27.13 NRSV) and in the world of the truly alive for ever.

Copyright acknowledgements

Scripture quotations marked NRSV are from the New Revised Standard Version of the Bible, Anglicized Edition, copyright © 1989, 1995 by the Division of Christian Education of the National Council of the Churches of Christ in the USA. Used by permission. All rights reserved.

Quotations marked KJV are from the Authorized Version of the Bible (The King James Bible), the rights in which are vested in the Crown, and are reproduced by permission of the Crown's Patentee, Cambridge University Press.

All unacknowledged prayers are by the author. The publisher and author acknowledge with thanks permission to reproduce extracts from the following:

Extracts from The Book of Common Prayer, the rights in which are vested in the Crown, are reproduced by permission of the Crown's Patentee, Cambridge University Press. All psalm passages are from The Book of Common Prayer unless specifically marked otherwise.

Extract taken from the song 'How great thou art' by Stuart K. Hine: all rights worldwide admin by Kingsway Communications Ltd <tym@kingsway.co.uk> except USA admin by EMI CMG Publishing and print rights admin by Hope Publishing Company. All other rights in North, Central and South America admin by Manna Music Inc.

Every effort has been made to seek permission to use copyright material reproduced in this book. The publisher apologizes for those cases where permission might not have been sought and, if notified, will formally seek permission at the earliest opportunity.

13575698R00099

Printed in Great Britain
by Amazon.co.uk, Ltd.,
Marston Gate.